YOUR LIFE
IN 1990

CANCER

GW00721969

YOUR LIFE
IN 1990

CANCER

June 22 to July 22

ROGER ELLIOT

Futura

A Futura Book

Copyright © Roger Elliot 1989

First published in Great Britain in 1989
by Futura Publications, a Division of
Macdonald & Co (Publishers) Ltd
London & Sydney

All rights reserved.
No part of this publication may be reproduced,
stored in a retrieval system, or transmitted, in any
form or by any means without the prior
permission in writing of the publisher, nor be
otherwise circulated in any form of binding or
cover other than that in which it is published and
without a similar condition including this
condition being imposed on the subsequent
purchaser

ISBN 0 7088 4271 2

Photoset in North Wales by
Derek Doyle and Associates, Mold, Clwyd,
from computer discs prepared by the author.
Printed and bound in Great Britain by
Hazell, Watson & Viney Limited
Member of BPCC Limited
Aylesbury, Bucks

Futura Publications
A Division of
Macdonald & Co (Publishers) Ltd
66-73 Shoe Lane
London EC4P 4AB

A member of Maxwell Pergamon Publishing Corporation plc

Contents

ROGER ELLIOT is one of the top astrologers in the world today. As a writer, TV performer, teacher and consultant to many individuals, he spans the full range of astrology from scientific research to newspaper columns.

He provides a comprehensive astrology telephone service in Britain called *Ask the Oracle*, which is also available in Australia and Hong Kong.

Roger, born on June 25 under the sign of Cancer, lives in a Somerset manor house with his blonde Leo wife Suzie, and two teenage children Stephanie (Aries) and Mark (Aquarius) – not forgetting the Sagittarian Jack Russell terrier Sebastian.

For information about Roger Elliot's Starlife astrology service, please write to Starlife, Cossington, Somerset TA7 8JR.

My World of Astrology

Welcome once again to my annual series of Zodiac books – this time for the start of the new decade, 1990 – and greetings to all my readers throughout the world.

It's a pleasure to indicate to you how the year ahead is likely to unfold. I think you have plenty to look forward to, although there are bound to be some setbacks and disappointments.

Remember that the daily forecasts are written in two sections. The first half, *written in italic*, refers to the whole world and everyone in it. They give you an idea how other people are likely to behave on the day in question – indeed, they may give a clue to the national and international events taking place.

The second half of each daily forecast refers, as usual, to yourself – as a birth-child of Cancer – and the moods, events and circumstances that may occur in your individual life. Sometimes they match the generalised forecast, but sometimes they differ, simply because the planets that day are making a special pattern as far as your Zodiac sign is concerned.

Once again I've included Wise Words at the end of each monthly group of predictions. Most of them are wry or funny, so don't take them all that seriously, but each of them does refer, however obliquely, to the mood of the month.

As before, the section Mixing with Others enables you to see how you relate to each of the twelve Zodiac signs. Perhaps it will help you to understand personal links more clearly, whether it's a friendship, a sexual partnership, a relative or business contact.

Astrology of this kind is a team effort, a combination of my expertise and your experience. Over the years I have developed a complex array of skills for examining the heavens. Using computers with vast memories, I can analyse the planetary movements with considerable finesse.

Modern astrology is akin to weather forecasting. Today's meteorologists use computers to compare wind and temperature patterns now with all the patterns of yesteryear. As a result, their forecasts are becoming more accurate. In just the same way, I do not simply use theory.

From my own observations, as well as your thousands of letters over the years, I have been able to compare the evidence of the stars with actual reality. Every time you tell me that, yes – on such and such a date you did indeed have a headache, or no – in that particular month you did not start a new job, it goes into the computer. (Please don't worry – everything is completely confidential between you and me.)

But your evidence, private though it is, becomes part of my public store of knowledge; and this year, more than ever, my 1990 predictions are based as much on your experiences in the past as on my intuition in reading the stars.

So keep on writing to me. I love hearing your news and finding out whether my predictions are true. The more feedback I get from you, the more accurate I can be.

The reason is, you see, that patterns in the sky repeat themselves, just as weather patterns do. Every time Venus forms an opposition to Saturn, say, there should be a similar kind of event in your life.

Obviously the precise circumstances will vary from one Cancer to the next. A teenager, unemployed in York, will experience the influence somewhat differently from a middle-aged businessman in New York. So you must always use common sense in interpreting my forecasts. Apply those words that are applicable. Ignore the remarks that clearly have no reference to your life.

Let me give you a fascinating example from my own life. A year or two ago, I suffered a heart attack – a small one, luckily, but still serious. As I recovered in hospital, I examined the planets to find out the astrological reason for this. Sure enough, I found that three planets – Mars, Saturn and Uranus – were exactly opposite the Sun in my horoscope, and square my Saturn: a clear indication of surprise, shock and bad news.

This planetary combination is rare but not unique, so I was interested to see when, in the past, the same planets made a similar impact on my horoscope. I found that in the fourth week of March 1981 both Mars and Saturn in the sky were exactly opposite my Saturn and square my Sun, while Uranus was exactly four signs away.

And what happened that week? My house burned down!

This stunning example that astrology really works raises some interesting points. I did not 'cause' either event; they were acts of fate that happened to me. Does that mean that the next time this planetary configuration occurs – in 1996 – I must willy-nilly put up with whatever fate hurls at me?

Or can I mitigate its effect? I believe I can – and should. Astrology gives clear warning of the happiness or sadness in store for us, but it's up to us to cool these influences, or encourage them, depending on what we want. I have learnt from my mistake. I knew, after all, about this impending 'heart-attack' warning, but had simply assumed that it would be a hard-working time. Because I did not cool the influence down – through relaxation and stress control – fate did it for me!

So bear this in mind as you read my forecasts for you. The real effect of the stars on your life may, in the end, be unavoidable; but you can still control how to respond.

I've tried my best in this book to give you fair warning of the influences ahead. But do remember that I'm always willing to help with your personal problems. If you want to learn more about astrology, and get your own horoscope in some way, write to me at Starlife, Cossington, Somerset TA7 8JR. Wherever you live, whatever your difficulties, your letter will reach me.

In the meantime, the world rolls round. With so much space travel nowadays, it's easy to visualise our little globe, a gleam of blue and white in a black universe, apparently the only sign of life amid an empty deadness. But it isn't really like that. We are surrounded by invisible forces, most of them wanting to nurture life and goodness on this planet.

Of course there is pain, sadness and death. But the life-force is inexorable. Touch the source of that energy, and you will be filled with a sense of joy and well-being and purpose.

May this Cancer book help you to widen your perspective and bring you closer to the source of all life.

God bless you, my friend.

ROGER ELLIOT

Technical
Note

Some people think that astrology is all psychic intuition, but it's a good deal more scientific than that.

First of all, using my computers, I prepare an *ephemeris* for 1990 listing the positions of the Sun and planets, together with all their midpoints, for each day of the year. They are grouped along a great circle in the sky called the *ecliptic* or Zodiac, which is divided into the twelve signs.

Then I prepare a daily *aspectarian* telling which planets are in line with each other, or in opposition, or square to each other, or whatever it may be. Let's take my own birthday as an example. On June 25 Mars is square Jupiter, while Mercury is quincunx Saturn. These are just two of fourteen aspects in force that day.

Now each planet represents a different quality in life. Mars stands for energy and enterprise, while Jupiter stands for happiness. So it's a broadly pleasant day, but the Mercury-Saturn contact means there will be some aggravation and arguments and disappointment.

That's why my general prediction for this day, as you can see on page 65 is *Quite a happy time, though there's a note of bullying in the air.* In fact, this combination could produce an international squabble.

The individual forecast that follows is based on a careful analysis of what these planets mean for Cancer. Sometimes I am very scientific, noting the rulerships of the planets as far as you are concerned, and sometimes I simply get a mental picture of the various conflicting forces and imagine how a person like yourself would respond.

So it's a mixture of science and imagination – I hope! At all events, I trust it will be helpful to you.

If you ever need a technical description of your own horoscope, looking at all the planets, write to me at the address on the previous page.

10

Mixing
with Others

You may think that just because you're a Cancer person you have got nothing in common with other Zodiac signs.

But in fact the twelve signs have a lot in common, because all the Zodiac signs are linked by an enthralling system of Elements and Modes. By discovering which Mode and Element you belong to, you can find out what you have in common with other signs – and what you don't!

Each sign belongs to one Mode and one Element. Naturally you get on well with other signs that share these qualities.

The Modes

Aries, Cancer, Libra and Capricorn belong to the **Cardinal Mode.** All the Cardinal signs are concerned with activity. In their differing ways they like to get things moving; to take practical steps; to start a new enterprise. So they resemble the cardinal points of the compass – north, south, east and west – in the sense that they point in a new direction.

Taurus, Leo, Scorpio and Aquarius all belong to the **Fixed Mode.** Fixed signs are exactly what they say they are: immovable and fixed, gaining strength from maintaining a situation rather than changing it. They have the virtue of persistence and the drawback of stubbornness.

If the Cardinal signs can be symbolised by a pointing finger, Fixed signs are represented by a clenched fist.

Gemini, Virgo, Sagittarius and Pisces belong to the **Mutable Mode.** Mutable signs express changeability. They are also called dualistic signs because their energy seems to fluctuate.

If Cardinal signs drive straight down the road, Mutable ones veer from side to side. This provides great flexibility of outlook, but also great unreliability and lack of constancy. Images like a flickering candle capture the basic Mutable quality.

The Elements

Capricorn, Taurus and Virgo belong to the **Earth** Element. Earth signs are solid, reliable and stable. The world tends to approve of earthy people, although they can be rather crude and indelicate at times. We like their common sense.

The drawback of these signs is their lack of enterprise and vision. They can become encased in materialism, and gradually action can become clogged by inertia.

Aries, Leo and Sagittarius belong to the **Fire** Element. All the Fire signs have a magical quality, enabling them to fire other people into activity. At their most creative, these signs have constant access to real enthusiasm. They are powered by an unending fuel store helping them to achieve a great deal. At their most destructive, however, the Fire signs use other people as fuel. They burn the energy out of them, leaving behind a trail of wrecked hearts.

Libra, Aquarius and Gemini belong to the **Air** Element. Air is an insubstantial Element. It breezes this way and that, carrying seeds from one part of the land to another. Traditionally it's linked with the transmission of ideas.

Air signs are communicative and sociable – bringing men and women together; spreading ideas and trying to change their surroundings. You can see the possible faults of these signs in the popular sayings 'too airy-fairy' or 'talking a lot of hot air'.

Cancer, Scorpio and Pisces belong to the **Water** Element. Water is the most mysterious of the four Elements. We are said to be born in the waters of the womb, or have evolved from earlier aquatic creatures, and spiritually we return to the great waters of eternity.

Water signs have a fine capacity to flow into the hearts and minds of other people. Like electricity through water, they are conducive to the ideas and feelings coming their way, and they respond very sensitively to their environment.

At worst, of course, they are wet, drippy and sloppy!

Aries
March 21 to April 20

Friendships Aries people like friends but hate to be dependent on them. They are self-reliant folk who, in the last resort, are quite happy on their own. They take friends at face value, and don't like people who are too moody or changeable or hanging back from making decisions. They enjoy the company of people who are enthusiastic, good-humoured and brave – just like themselves, in fact!

Sex Aries people are sexy, but that doesn't make them all Don Juans or nymphomaniacs. They have a strong, muscular sex nature that likes to impose itself on others. If anything, their sexuality is stronger than their need for love. Certainly they are self-centred people, and can ignore their partners' feelings.

Marriage Aries folk are not settlers by nature, but more like nomads or hunters. There's more fun for them in making new conquests than sticking with the same old mate. On the other hand, they hate failure – and what they have, they hold. So they can make loyal, stable marriage partners. If the marriage does get stale, Aries is the one to put a stop to the agony.

Aries (March 21 to April 20) and You

Aries seems to be boss, but Cancer wins in the end!
You look for a tender relationship. Is Aries too crude?

An **Aries friend** is self-centred and active, and tempestuous at times. You go on the defensive. Together you can achieve plenty. 1990 rating: don't invade each other's privacy too much.

With an **Aries parent** you will be told exactly what to do in a blunt but honest way. You'll tend to retreat into your shell. 1990 rating: great, provided you don't see too much of each other!

If you have an **Aries child** you're inclined to be too

13

possessive and perhaps disapproving about your child's life-style. 1990 rating: competitive, especially if you share the same hobby.

An **Aries boy-friend** is not as considerate as you'd like. He's macho and tough, but sometimes blind to other people's feelings. 1990 rating: better than average.

An **Aries girl-friend** is active, go-getting and candid – more so than you welcome. In each other you find what you lack in yourself. 1990 rating: warm, then rapidly cooling.

An **Aries husband** is a good choice, as he's very masculine and you're very feminine. An old-fashioned, unliberated union. 1990 rating: could be a third party involved.

An **Aries wife** will keep you busy at home and work, driving you hard – and maybe driving you crazy in the end! Great if you can stand the pace. 1990 rating: some verbal battles.

If your **Aries boss** has a fault, it's watching the clock. You prefer a more relaxed attitude. 1990 rating: promotion beckons – for both of you. The future looks good.

Taurus
April 21 to May 21

Friendship Taurean people are among the most gregarious folk in the Zodiac. They love being surrounded by friends, and seek to form firm, solid friendships that last forever. It's part of the deep Taurean need for security. But there's a generous side to the bargain as well. They love plying their friends with food and drink, making them feel at home.

Sex Taurus is one of the sexiest of Zodiac signs. There is a basic earthiness about their approach to sex. They love living in their own bodies and, through kissing and touching, making contact with a loved one's body. They are highly sensual, and the danger is they'll make sex the be-all and end-all of their relationships. If the body loses appeal, they lose interest. A Taurean can too often take the partner's feelings for granted.

Marriage Taureans are made for marriage. It's the most

14

natural way for them to live, sharing with another and building up a strong, mutually supportive family. Ideally they are monogamist by nature, and want to stay faithful. They feel secure within marriage, and would only stray for sexual gratification. Otherwise they make loyal spouses.

Taurus (April 21 to May 21) and You

Both are family-oriented people who want to settle down, gradually merging with each other as the years pass.

A **Taurus friend** is a warm, reliable creature, great to have around in hard times. You suit each other splendidly, and the friendship should last for life. 1990 rating: amiable.

A **Taurus parent** is watchful and loving but wants you to tow the line. You are much more imaginative, and want to dream! 1990 rating: you must cheer him or her up.

A **Taurus child** can develop close, almost telepathic ties with you. In a family crisis, you're the ones to stand firm. 1990 rating: bouncy when the good news comes – which it will. Lots in common this year.

A **Taurus boy-friend** will seem right at the start. There's a wonderful flow of empathy between you. Both are looking for marriage. 1990 rating: plain stubborn at times.

A **Taurus girl-friend** is ideal for you. Once you get in a steady routine, nothing will budge you. Faithfulness counts for a great deal. 1990 rating: enjoy her best qualities, as this can be a very physical relationship.

A **Taurus husband** is a great partner for you and a wonderful father to your children. This is a family-minded marriage, never roaming far from home. 1990 rating: quietly encouraging year. Less aggro than in the past.

A **Taurus wife** is one of the best choices you can make. You will become a conservative couple, growing more like each other as the years pass. 1990 rating: good progress made.

With a **Taurus boss** you can work really hard, without getting bored with each other. 1990 rating: there will be plenty of consultation, but in the end he's still the boss – and don't you forget it!

Gemini
May 22 to June 21

Friendship Geminians are the most friendly people in the Zodiac, though, to be honest, they are better at making casual acquaintances than deep personal ties. One reason is that people find them an attractive type, easy to be with, because they have the gift of adapting themselves to suit the company. But they are fair-weather friends. If trouble looms, they don't want to know.

Sex Gemini people talk themselves into and out of love, almost as though it were a game. Gemini is not a highly-sexed sign, even though they may have plenty of sexual experience. Instead, sex for them is a rather special form of conversation. It does not necessarily involve them in deep feelings. But it's quite possible for Geminians to enjoy non-sexual relationships.

Marriage As Gemini is the most devious, two-faced and freewheeling of all Zodiac signs, it follows that marriage is not really suited to their nature. But they can still make a success of marriage. They need a partner who can keep them on their toes; who can spring surprises; who is more a lover than a spouse; and who, if necessary, can turn a blind eye every time they stray.

Gemini (May 22 to June 21) and You

You are very different people, with Gemini lively but tricky while you are sensitive, sincere and heartfelt.

A **Gemini friend** is a marvellously entertaining companion, but not the type you become very close to. Gemini always makes you feel young-at-heart. 1990 rating: enterprising.

If you have a **Gemini parent** I'm afraid you'll find him or her rather impatient. But there'll be lots of fun and holidays. 1990 rating: happily going elsewhere.

With a **Gemini child** your parental care and sympathy

16

won't be much appreciated. So you have a youngster who wants to be free. 1990 rating: hot and bothered at times, but not destructive.

A **Gemini boy-friend** will woo you quickly, but may break off the affair quickly, too. He's great company, but isn't as faithful as you'd like. 1990 rating: there may not be enough interest to keep it going.

A **Gemini girl-friend** is a good-humoured partner. But she's the fickle type. The more you cling, the faster she'll run. 1990 rating: you will see life in different ways.

A **Gemini husband** will be good with kids, but he lacks your own homespun sympathy. Can you trust him when he's away? 1990 rating: better relations and greater understanding.

A **Gemini wife** may not be as motherly as you'd like. But she is lively, inquisitive and full of fun. She'll keep you on your toes. 1990 rating: she wants to run the marriage herself.

A **Gemini boss** is an ideas man, but he doesn't take human feelings sufficiently into account. 1990 rating: a good accord, but the time is approaching when you must willy-nilly part.

Cancer
June 22 to July 22

Friendship Cancerians are clannish people at the best of times. They want to be friendly, but they can't help being suspicious of strangers at first. Once they've decided to make someone a friend, they tend to adopt them completely, drawing them into the family, so to speak. Cancerians have a great ability to identify with their friends' feelings, and love sharing.

Sex Although shy at first, Cancer folk soon fall hook, line and sinker for the right sweetheart. They're terrible clingers, hanging on for dear life if a lover seems to be losing interest. Sexually they have access to deep, ecstatic feelings. Physical pleasure is nothing compared with the spiritual orgasms they are capable of experiencing. Cancerians never forget a former sweetheart, and still feel possessive after many years.

Marriage Cancerians are born to be married. They want to share their life with the perfect partner. Cancer men have a good deal of tenderness in their natures; they like strong-minded women who will look after them – indeed, mother them. Cancer women are very feminine, and need men who are kind, loyal and humorous – in short, a homely chap.

Cancer (June 22 to July 22) and You

This can be a wonderful relationship between two like-minded people – but your moods can get you down!

A **Cancer friend** will be like a brother or sister. You have lots in common, but it's a private friendship, flourishing on its own. 1990 rating: more promising this year.

A **Cancer parent** has obviously left an indelible impression, for better or worse, on your psyche. 1990 rating: great!

A **Cancer child** picks up many of your thoughts and feelings. You can be close, yet you both know how to hurt each other. 1990 rating: home surroundings are cramped.

A **Cancer boy-friend** will take wonderful care of you. But he'll be jealous of you at times, and will hate to share you with others. 1990 rating: fine, especially if you meet for the first time this year.

A **Cancer girl-friend** is looking for a home and family, and will want to settle down with you. Better when you're both a bit older. 1990 rating: it should be a loving year.

A **Cancer husband** will want to run the house in his own way. He'll compare you with his mother – not always favourably. 1990 rating: a year of slight upsets.

With a **Cancer wife** you form a very maternal household, with lots of role-swapping. A soft, gentle couple – though you pick up each other's moods. 1990 rating: a nice sociable year.

If you have a **Cancer boss** you see business problems too much from the same point of view. 1990 rating: busy but unsatisfying. You may part before the end of the year.

Leo
July 23 to August 23

Friendship All Leo folk thrive on friendship, but Leo likes to be the dominant partner. They want to be flattered, praised, loved and enjoyed – that's what friendship means to them. But that isn't all. For a Leo, the heart will always rule the head. They would do anything for a friend – indeed, they would put friendship above all.

Sex There's only one thing to do on a hot afternoon – and that is to make love! So think Leo people, anyway. Nothing pleases them more than someone of the opposite sex making eyes at them. They love to be wooed. Falling in love comes very naturally to Leo folk. It's probably true to say that a Leo can't feel truly fulfilled without a good sex life.

Marriage Leos may enjoy flirting at parties, but in the end they are looking for a steady marriage. They need courtship and security at the same time. If ever a marriage breaks up, it can shatter the Leo heart – and like a broken mirror it never quite recovers. A Leo man needs a warmly responsive wife, while the Leo woman wants fidelity and affection.

Leo (July 23 to August 23) and You

A classic combination in the whole Zodiac.
Leos are vain and bossy, but you can calm them down.

A **Leo friend** basically wants a companion who is full of fun and gaiety. You worry more than he does. There's a nice flow of feelings between you. 1990 rating: some problems you can face together.

A **Leo parent** should have been someone you always admired. This is an excellent combination, and you should love each other. 1990 rating: family problems bring you closer together.

With a **Leo child** you must be patient, good-humoured, full of fun yourself – and strict about money! 1990 rating: could be the start of a new chapter in this relationship.

A **Leo boy-friend** is a glorious lover in the right mood. But he needs to be humoured and flattered first. He wants all the attention at parties! 1990 rating: sex can become mechanical. But there's great initial attraction.

A **Leo girl-friend** makes you glad to be alive. In return, she'll want you to worship her. Never say she's ageing! A very male-female relationship. 1990 rating: loving, but she's selfish.

A **Leo husband** is an ideal choice, if you're an old-fashioned girl whose place is in the home. He will be the head of the family all right. 1990 rating: terrific once you know each other.

A **Leo wife** dislikes housework, and sees kids as an adornment to herself. But she's wonderful company, so long as you don't pour cold water on her plans. 1990 rating: you need courage to say goodbye to the past.

A **Leo boss** is Mr Big Deal. Flatter him like mad, but keep your real thoughts to yourself! 1990 rating: a steady year, without much to show for it.

Virgo
August 24 to September 22

Friendship Virgo people distrust strangers. When they meet a new person, they're distant at first. Only when they feel safe will they relax and become more personal. Even then, they are not as friendly as most Zodiac signs. They don't mix as freely, and are much more choosy about friends. They like people who are kindly, intelligent and observant – like themselves.

Sex Traditionally Virgo is the least sexy of all the Zodiac. Virgo people are capable of strong platonic friendships, and they don't seem to need sex as much as other people. Perhaps they need awakening – and once they realise how exciting it can be, they enjoy a splendid sex life. Some Virgoans, particularly women, put themselves on a pedestal, pretending to be far too good for the opposite sex.

Marriage Virgoans tend to remain unmarried longer than other signs. They need space to themselves, where they can be private. Virgoan men need a strong-minded wife who won't be too domineering. He needs someone who will give him enthusiasm as well as encouragement. Virgoan women look for emotional security. They are the kind to have a career outside marriage.

Virgo (August 24 to September 22) and You

You share an interest in money and home life,
but Virgo is a bit too fussy and dry for you.

A **Virgo friend** is a placid creature, expecting you to supply emotional excitement. Virgo can be an awful critic, which you could take to heart. 1990 rating: you are competitive.

A **Virgo parent** will have given you a sensible, middle-of-the-road upbringing. You share many qualities in common, and should relate well. 1990 rating: temper and high spirits.

A **Virgo child** is someone who strives hard, but is not the pushy type. A gentle prod from you won't come amiss. 1990 rating: you can certainly be encouraging.

A **Virgo boy-friend** is clever in bed, though he seems to turn his passion on and off like a tap. You'll wonder if you're really getting through to him. 1990 rating: sexy and lasting!

A **Virgo girl-friend** has a cutting edge that you don't like. But otherwise she's a homely creature, and you could well make wedding plans. 1990 rating: she's looking for security.

A **Virgo husband** is a perfect marriage partner for you: mild, loving and a credit to the neighbourhood! Sometimes you'll want more passion, though. 1990 rating: wonderful!

A **Virgo wife** is a classic combination with Cancer. You should last a lifetime together. It's a quiet marriage, but with plenty of quiet strength. 1990 rating: a clash.

A **Virgo boss** is efficient but nervous. It could be a tidy-minded working relationship. 1990 rating: charming and positive. You should enjoy working together.

Libra
September 23 to October

Friendship Librans thrive on friendship – more than any other Zodiac sign. Without friends they feel lost, only half-alive, for they are so amicable themselves. They mix easily, but can quickly detect if someone is 'not nice'. They adore small talk, chats on the phone, and social gatherings of all kinds. They have the rare ability to stay in touch with childhood friends.

Sex Librans are made for loving! They are one of those Zodiac signs who do distinguish between sex and love. Love without sex is okay, but sex without love is abhorrent. In the right relationship, they want to share themselves, body and soul, with the person they love. They are the psychological type who is drawn to their opposite – not always a good thing!

Marriage Of all Zodiac signs, Libra is the one most suited to marriage. They seem to be born as 'twin souls', and spend their lives looking for the ideal mate. Librans of both sexes need someone who is a good pal as well as lover. Libran men need an organised woman who isn't bossy. Libran women feel they need a real macho man who will look after them forever.

Libra (September 23 to October 23) and You

*One of the pleasantest combinations –
just the right emotional tension and sympathy.*

A **Libra friend** will be perfectly friendly, but don't expect him to take the lead. You will be one of many acquaintances. 1990 rating: you are clever together.

From a **Libra parent** you receive loving kindness, but not necessarily the push you need to get ahead. A sweet, comfy and undemanding relationship. 1990 rating: enjoyable most of the time.

A **Libra child** is easy-going, but lacks strong motivation.

Encourage, but don't interfere too much. Enjoy this child's charm. 1990 rating: an awkward phase.

A **Libra boy-friend** is full of romance, but a bit shy. So are you, so I hope you eventually manage to get together! 1990 rating: one of you is looking for someone new.

A **Libra girl-friend** wants to put herself out to please you. You make a super couple, and everyone will say you should get married. 1990 rating: five out of ten – but it could improve.

A **Libra husband** is a soft-hearted chap who'll do anything to keep you happy. Charm him, and you've got a lovely hubby. 1990 rating: let him speak up for himself.

A **Libra wife** is a bit lazy around the house, and prefers a party to a chat round the fire. You're a nice couple. She wants you to take the lead. 1990 rating: quarrels, but they're patched up. Some emotional blackmail.

With a **Libra boss** you have a friendly, homely relationship. 1990 rating: getting slowly better, especially from April onwards.

Scorpio
October 24 to November 22

Friendship Scorpio people are highly suspicious of newcomers. They don't make friends easily, and they can test their friendships so severely that they frighten would-be pals away. But once a true friendship is formed, it lasts for life. As far as Scorpio is concerned, friendship is a matter of utter loyalty. Friendship with members of their own sex is very important.

Sex Sex is a deeper, richer experience for Scorpio than perhaps for anyone else. At the same time, they manage to make sex far more complex and meaningful than it need be. Many Scorpians are frightened of sexual power. Raw sex, without love, worries them more than most people. It's certainly hard for them to have a casual, lightweight affair. As in so many other aspects of their lives, it's all or nothing.

Marriage Scorpians don't take their marriage vows lightly.

They mean to keep them, through bad times as well as good. They can be very jealous if slighted, but within a happy relationship they are the happiest of partners, for they are capable of much devotion. Scorpio men need a woman who can be a real soul-mate. Scorpio women need a strong man – the tougher the better.

Scorpio (October 24 to November 22) and You

This is a fierce, loyal, make-or-break relationship.
It can produce ecstatic – or disastrous – results.

A **Scorpio friend** is an enigma to start with. But it soon becomes an all-or-nothing liaison. You feel inevitably drawn together. 1990 rating: good all round – excellent company, loyal friend.

A **Scorpio parent** has deep emotional links with you, for better or worse. You can't wash this person out of your life – not easily, anyhow. 1990 rating: excellent between grown-ups.

A **Scorpio child** has a similar emotional set-up to yourself, though he's better at keeping feelings to himself. 1990 rating: needs encouragement in love, so don't seem cold.

A **Scorpio boy-friend** can pierce your innermost soul with passion and caring. Equally he can be the biggest bastard on earth! 1990 rating: fine in short bursts.

A **Scorpio girl-friend** has a marvellous sexuality, once you've awakened her. There may be a skeleton in the cupboard she hasn't told you about. 1990 rating: could be a split-up.

A **Scorpio husband** makes big demands on your time, patience and emotional stamina. But if you love him, you don't mind. 1990 rating: a good match, getting better now.

A **Scorpio wife** provides a passionate marriage, though you can keep secrets from each other. Rows a-plenty with some marvellous reconciliations. 1990 rating: you've got lots to give.

A **Scorpio boss** will criticise your work – but secretly he admires you more than he lets on. 1990 rating: more like partners than boss and employee.

24

Sagittarius
November 23 to December 21

Friendship Sagittarians are friendly – for a while – but people cannot rely on them. They can drop friends as easily as they can pick them up – without much heartbreak. Most Sagittarians have a built-in charm that never fails to attract. There's a relaxed, informal manner which doesn't really look for lasting links. They like new people, so old pals are taken for granted.

Sex They have a very flirtatious manner that enjoys chatting up the opposite sex. There's also an element of victory involved. They like to win hearts, and at times they get a thrill from leaving a broken heart by the wayside. Sagittarians enjoy sex on impulse, perhaps in exotic locations! They can get bored with the sameness of love-making with the same old partner!

Marriage Sagittarians are not the most monogamous of people. It's hard for them to maintain interest in one person all their lives. So they need partners who have the same variety-seeking outlook on life that Sagittarians have. Men born under Sagittarius appreciate a woman with a mind of her own. Sagittarian women respond to real men, full of zest for life.

Sagittarius (November 23 to December 21) and You

It's a strange mixture – you so sensitive and home-loving, and Sagittarius lively and travelling. It can still work.

A **Sagittarius friend** is like a breath of fresh air in your life: here today and gone tomorrow, but a wonderful passing influence. 1990 rating: very positive, cheerful.

With a **Sagittarius parent** you have a lively individual who won't have 'mothered' you as cosily as you'd have liked. 1990 rating: encourage the best qualities in each of you.

A **Sagittarius child** should be the apple of your eye – sporty, adventurous, doing all the things you were scared to do as a child! 1990 rating: some arguments.

A **Sagittarius boy-friend** loves conquering women – then moving on for the next kill. Enjoy him while you've got him. Expect friendly arguments. 1990 rating: he's passing through a complex phase.

A **Sagittarius girl-friend** is drawn to you because you have qualities she lacks. So be yourself, but recognise how different you are. 1990 rating: sexually alluring, but you may still not suit each other.

A **Sagittarius husband** is his own man, and can't be hen-pecked. He'll be a good husband, so long as he has some freedom. 1990 rating: you may lose a little respect for him.

A **Sagittarius wife** hates to be cooped up at home with nothing to do. If you try to restrain her, she'll up and leave. 1990 rating: you may lose interest for a while.

A **Sagittarius boss** loves arguments and discussions, so don't keep ideas to yourself. 1990 rating: enjoy yourselves, but recognise that you have quite different personalities.

Capricorn
December 22 to January 20

Friendship Capricorn folk make friends with difficulty – but once made, they tend to remain friends for life. The wall around the Capricorn heart makes it hard for us to get to know them well. Friendship for the Capricorn type is not a light-hearted, take-it-or-leave-it affair. It must be based on real virtues such as trust, honour and the readiness to help.

Sex Capricorn people have such a cold manner at times that they appear unsexy. Actually they are highly sexed, though it does not always flow out in a harmonious way. They are not flirty types. They adopt a serious approach to life, and can turn nasty and jealous if slighted. Yet their planet Saturn is linked to the old Roman orgies, so they can certainly let themselves go! They can turn from frost to warmth in a split second!

Marriage Marriage is a solemn matter to Capricorn folk. They intend to make it last for life. Once married, they feel they own their partners. They don't look for freedom or adventure. All their energies are devoted to maintaining the marriage as it is. This can lead to a stale situation where they take their spouses too much for granted.

Capricorn (December 22 to January 20) and You

You suit each other, because you both believe in home, family and tradition. But Capricorn can be cold at times.

A **Capricorn friend** has great strength of character, which attracts you. You can stay friends for life, though Capricorn isn't as heart-felt as you. 1990 rating: edgy and critical.

With a **Capricorn parent** you have deep ties, but these are not always comfortable. You may feel restrained by this parent. 1990 rating: as you get older, you want to take charge of this relative.

A **Capricorn child** relies on you a great deal, more than you realise. Steady support and encouragement are needed. 1990 rating: you're very sensitive together for good or bad.

A **Capricorn boy-friend** can be cold – but once you've warmed him up, he'll be an astute lover, fond and conscientious. 1990 rating: he's shy, so needs encouraging.

A **Capricorn girl-friend** can be an ice princess to start with. This friendship takes time to develop. She will organise your life for you. 1990 rating: she's in two minds. Push her, and she'll run away.

A **Capricorn husband** is a dignified father and marriage partner. Very traditional in outlook, he's a man you can respect. 1990 rating: kindliness, and the ability to say sorry.

A **Capricorn wife** may be shy to start with, but in the end she'll run the marriage. A long-lasting match. 1990 rating: very positive and successful.

A **Capricorn boss** can form a firm, no-nonsense link with you. 1990 rating: if you've recently got together, there's a lot of hope for the future.

Aquarius
January 21 to February 18

Friendship Friendships mean much to Aquarians. At the same time they want to remain independent. So they are friendly with lots of people, but always slightly stand-offish – as if they are really on their own. Aquarians are good at making and keeping friends. Primarily they are interested in mental friendship – the rapport between people who share the same interests.

Sex Aquarius is one of three signs (Gemini and Virgo are the others) that are not obviously sexual. Don't worry, they can have a perfectly normal and happy love life; but they treat people as humans first, and as sexual partners only later. They are capable of great tenderness. But a passionate partner will say they don't get sufficiently involved.

Marriage Aquarians see their partners as equals – not people who must be dominated or obeyed. At the same time they're freedom-loving in outlook, so it's difficult for them to share the little things in life. They need emotional elbow-room, and hate to be owned or trapped. Aquarians are rarely the unhappy victims of marriage. If it breaks up, Aquarians go first.

Aquarius (January 21 to February 18) and You

Not the easiest of companions. You won't find the emotional rapport you crave, and Aquarius is too independent.

An **Aquarius friend** appeals to your idealism. He's not really reliable, and you'll constantly wonder how firm the friendship really is. 1990 rating: slightly nit-picking and critical.

An **Aquarius parent** will not have been the solid support you wanted when young. Now you're older there is a better relationship. 1990 rating: you can forge deep links this year, better than ever.

28

An **Aquarius child** is a modern youngster, a bit quirky and unusual, with whom you don't always see eye to eye. 1990 rating: trust and tolerance are called for.

An **Aquarius boy-friend** wants an equal partner, so don't imagine he will squash the life out of you. You'll wish he would get more committed. 1990 rating: you are likely to slip apart.

An **Aquarius girl-friend** is cool, quirky, independent – not the cosy bed-mate you really want. There's an attraction for a while. 1990 rating: you'll both have fun, but you aren't very faithful to each other.

An **Aquarius husband** will give you the possessions you want, but where's the emotional security? He likes the illusion of freedom. 1990 rating: more reassuring than recently.

An **Aquarius wife** hates to be cast in a mould. She isn't nearly such a good home-maker as yourself! She likes to be out and about. 1990 rating: love her, and she'll love you back.

With an **Aquarius boss** you have a nonconformist who likes to go his own way. 1990 rating: there could be promotion for you.

Pisces
February 19 to March 20

Friendship Pisceans are friendly folk. They enjoy meeting new people and can quickly become dependent on new friends – for love, loyalty and, if need be, support if things go wrong. At the same time they don't like to be 'owned', and get frustrated if chums try to organise their lives too much. Piscean men relate well to women, but Piscean women may be in awe of clever male friends.

Sex The Piscean aim in love is to achieve a wonderful, yielding rapport with their partners. They want to melt into love-making, losing their own identity. All the same, Pisceans are fussy in choosing the right partner. Because their imagination is powerful, they can see a would-be sexual partner in a rosy-coloured light, and can be terribly let down later. Sex without love does not suit the Piscean at all.

Marriage Pisceans have an ambiguous attitude towards marriage. In one way, their whole impulse is to make someone else happy and fulfilled. At the same time, they need to feel free. They should not marry someone who will be too possessive. Piscean men look for a woman who will take the lead in the marriage. Piscean women can be misused by an over-dominant husband.

Pisces (February 19 to March 20) and You

You flow into each other's hearts with great ease.
It's a union of empathy and succour.

A **Pisces friend** is a warm, amiable pal who will weep for your sorrows and smile with your joys. An over-emotional union, in other words. 1990 rating: a firm friendship can grow.

A **Pisces parent** was perfect for you – sympathetic and kindly. 1990 rating: fine, but give each other room.

A **Pisces child** can live in a dream-world of his own. There are many subtle links binding you together – not always comfortably. 1990 rating: good at times, but he or she is mischievous.

A **Pisces boy-friend** will adore you from afar, but may not have the courage to make a pass at you. So take the plunge yourself. 1990 rating: a parting of the ways?

A **Pisces girl-friend** makes you glad to be alive. She's all woman, and makes you believe you're all man! You can both get moods, and sulk. 1990 rating: needs more work put into it.

A **Pisces husband** may not give you the strength of purpose you want from a man. You'll have to nurse him along. 1990 rating: don't expect him to be as monogamous as yourself.

A **Pisces wife** is a good choice as a marriage partner. She will be a devoted wife so long as you treat her right! 1990 rating: promising, after a sticky patch.

From a **Pisces boss** you receive kindness and courtesy, though he's an inveterate muddler. 1990 rating: you're his anchor, and he'll rely greatly on you.

Your
Birthday Message

*This book applies to everyone born between
June 22 and July 22. But here, just for you,
is a special word of hope or caution,
depending on your actual birthday in Cancer.
Here is your own astrological message
to guide you through the year ahead.*

JUNE

Friday 22nd: A muddled year in some ways. You don't know where you stand in a relationship. Experts or officialdom could let you down.

Saturday 23rd: A fast-moving year. You will be travelling more than usual. There is happy family news. A romance may falter, then come back strongly.

Sunday 24th: Not an entirely happy year. You're in an escapist mood, and could be getting involved with someone new, knowing it won't last. But quite a hard-working year.

Monday 25th: A year when you must take care. Someone you trust could want to hurt you. Business partnerships may not go well. A time when you want to be independent.

Tuesday 26th: Excellent year for turning over a new leaf – and succeeding. A good year for re-organising your life in a more efficient way.

Wednesday 27th: Anything to do with travel, moving house, etc, is favoured. Time to tackle a new job or enjoy a one-in-a-lifetime holiday. Romance is definitely favoured.

Thursday 28th: Quite a lucky year. Good time for improving your home. A relationship that has been dodgy will now be much easier to cope with. You are lucky abroad.

Friday 29th: You may make a false start, and have to begin again. A nice year for romance in the short term, but don't expect it to last for ever. Health looks good.

Saturday 30th: A difficult task will be quite easy, once you have started. Quite a happy time. There may be a little

31

ill-health, but not enough to worry you.

JULY

Sunday 1st: A dream will move nearer reality. A bouncy year, full of vim and vigour. One small joy will lead to another. Luck comes in the springtime months.

Monday 2nd: A sentimental start to the year. Romance will flourish in the most unlikely circumstances. In mid-1990 you get a brilliant opportunity in terms of career.

Tuesday 3rd: Quite a sociable time. You can't wriggle out of a duty or promise you have made. Money problems will continue, I fear. A relationship improves no end.

Wednesday 4th: A disagreement will be carried out in a friendly manner. You could pick up someone else's bright idea and make it profitable. You will enjoy your spare time, especially in sport.

Thursday 5th: A year when you worry about other people's cash problems. There could be trouble to do with electricity. A practical year, with not much leisure time.

Friday 6th: A clear-minded time. You can see problems which other people are ignoring. Quite exuberant in love, so a new romance could blossom.

Saturday 7th: You must pause and consider where you are going. You will be lucky with a risk. One person will try to hold you back, but you are determined.

Sunday 8th: A reasonably sensible year – not exactly lucky, but you will avoid disaster. Something you never considered possible will start becoming a probability.

Monday 9th: A good time if you are at all artistic. A setback will make you moody for a while, but the overall outlook is good. Be lucky!

Tuesday 10th: You must make a compromise, especially if dealing with a strong-minded person. You will share a success. Quite a warm and sexy year.

Wednesday 11th: A quiet year in the family. You are more sentimental than usual. Good for bridging gaps, mending fences. But there's quite a touch of glamour, too.

Thursday 12th: You'll feel lucky, and will have something to

32

celebrate. A special hobby goes well. You will make extra money, but romance is not so favoured.

Friday 13th: Quite lucky. You will travel more than usual. You are deeply drawn to the past. There is more beauty in your life. Career chances are there, if you are ambitious.

Saturday 14th: Good time to start a new business. A new romance will excite you. A very shrewd year, though some people will find you're getting cold-hearted.

Sunday 15th: A hard-pressed year. There will be one or two moments of bad luck, but with perseverance you can succeed. A year of facts, not fancies.

Monday 16th: Something in your life is drawing to a close. Time to move on to a new venture. Some hopes will be dashed, but there's hope at the end of the tunnel.

Tuesday 17th: Frisky year. You'll be looking for new outlets. You may feel poorly in mid-year, but it's a good time to move house. You're lucky in the autumn months.

Wednesday 18th: A wonderful time, especially if you're a man. Cancer women could well have a new love. Full of zest, energy and success. You're on the ball, ready for anything.

Thursday 19th: Hard-working time. If you're elderly, there could be some loss of mobility. You will be popular company. There's plenty you can achieve.

Friday 20th: One of your better years. You will be popular and charming. A restless time, but others may not be helpful, even though they like you.

Saturday 21st: Busier than usual. You have lots on your plate, including a special honour. Domestic re-arrangements likely. A constructive year, good for growing families.

Sunday 22nd: You'll bump into old friends, and meet new ones too. Your partner has a change of mind, which you dislike. The family should be strong and healthy, and you make good progress in a job.

Your Decade
Ahead

At the start of the 1990s it's tempting to look ahead at the way the stars will broadly affect you in the decade ahead.

During most of **1991** the lucky planet Jupiter will be in Leo. Saturn moves into Aquarius. This looks marvellous for making money, but there may be a cloud over your sex life.

In **1992** Jupiter moves into Virgo, while Mars spends a long time in Cancer. You seem steamed up about something personal – so a hot and bothered year in prospect. But luck comes from other relatives – especially a brother or sister.

1993 sees Jupiter in Libra. This promises a happier home life, with perhaps a lovely house move. Links between parents and children are strong, and you can make a profit on property.

The following year, **1994**, finds Jupiter in Scorpio and Saturn in Pisces. Children could bring much happiness. You seem more responsible but close-knit, not wanting to move far afield. Despite all this, there could be a love affair.

1995 finds Jupiter in its own sign of Sagittarius. This will turn you into a happy workaholic, busy at lots of tasks.

The slow-moving planet Pluto moves properly into Sagittarius in **1996**, while Jupiter enters Capricorn. Single Cancerians may be faced by the possibility of marriage – but there's the threat of ill-health, too.

In **1997** the explosive planet Uranus enters its own sign of Aquarius, along with Jupiter. This does suggest the strong possibility of a surprise financial gain – one that could change your life completely.

Saturn spends half of **1998** in Aries, half in Taurus, with Jupiter in Pisces. It's a serious, responsible year at work, with increased foreign travel promised.

Finally, in the last year of the millenium, **1999**, Neptune moves into the New Age sign of Aquarius. The world will be transformed, perhaps by a new religion. There could be a puzzle over a lump-sum meant to be coming your way.

34

Your Year
Ahead

You may be looking for help at the start of the New Year, but it won't arrive on time. There could be problems at work, but there's good rapport with friends and neighbours even if you're feeling a bit selfish in love. In February you seem worried about something which may never happen, and March is a stop-go sort of time, when you make a good resolution only to break it. This is a good month to get in touch with old friends, and your love life certainly livens up.

You remain good-humoured and happy through much of April, and there may be a new business idea which is cheering you up. There will be some nice evenings out, but you may be a bit worried about romance.

May seems an exciting time when opportunities start to develop nicely. You may be out of pocket due to someone else's mistake, but there's a lot of hot passion in your life.

June continues the good work of May, but July seems more hesitant, especially where a job change is concerned. It's a great month for travel, and it also seems a loving time within a good marriage.

August is mixed, and in several ways you could be trying too hard. A sweetheart could give you a rough time, for instance.

September starts downbeat, then you relax more, but I'm afraid you become anxious and fretful again in October. The greatest area of worry could be to do with your career. You may wonder whether your job will last, or whether you should take a risky move away from a regular job.

November seems much better, as though the tide has turned. You will have made the right choice, and everything looks rosy from now on.

You will delight in the good things of life, and feel more confident about the future. You end the year in high spirits – hard-working but good-humoured and ready to look forward to 1991.

January
Guide

You may be looking for help at the start of the New Year, but it may not arrive on time. To some extent you'll feel left in the lurch, having to cope on your own for a while.

It's hard to say exactly in which area this will operate, but circumstances are changing for you around now – and it's important that your attitude changes, too. In other words you are being egged on by Fate to take a deep breath, look at yourself and others in a new light, and alter your opinions.

As always with a Cancerian, you are inclined to be a bit backward-looking, not to say nostalgic. Probably the changes mean that you must bring yourself more up-to-date, and accustom yourself to new surroundings.

WORK. This could be occurring in the work field, for instance. There may be new equipment to operate, new management to cope with, or a fresh product to sell. Whatever it is, you're inclined to be a bit slower than others.

If you are involved in business negotiations, you may not realise that your case is stronger than you thought, and you have a good chance of succeeding.

HOME. There is a note of sadness in your domestic surroundings. Something – or possibly someone – could have come to the end of its natural life. I'm thinking more of an old pet than a person, and, even more likely, an old washing machine or something like that!

Perhaps repairs that you've been putting off for a long time will now become urgent. Perhaps, too, a child's misbehaviour that you have tolerated until now is going to have to be corrected, once and for all.

HEALTH. You could be dealing more with someone with a disability, either at home or work or in your social scene. If so, do it with a glad heart, because you will learn plenty yourself about how limiting such problems can be.

No big problems on the health front, except for menopausal difficulties for some Cancer women and mild complications for some Cancer mums-to-be.

It's possible that a problem from last year will recur now. A broken bone, for instance, might have to be re-set.

MONEY. You will be very careful with money this month. It's a thrifty time, not only because it's that time of year, but also because you are in a money-hoarding mood.

You may keep some people waiting so long for a bill to be paid that they'll threaten legal action. But there can also be a dispute over a bill.

For a number of Cancer people there could be a looming repair bill on a car, house or furniture.

LEISURE. There's quite good rapport with friends and neighbours, and if you normally hibernate this month you'll be surprised at how sociable you can be. The Christmas party season seems to extend well into January, especially for people who were away over the holiday itself.

It's a good month, too, to get your head down to some reading, educational studies, home-based crafts and such like. It's also a good month for dealing with youngsters, especially passing on a skill you know well.

Watch out for: one marvellous weekend spent among the bright lights; a sports occasion that involves a coincidence and history repeating itself; a charity do where everyone enjoys themselves; and worry about pets, especially if you're away.

LOVE. Although you're not in a wildly giving mood, nor are you in a selfish, self-centred one. Ideally you'll have a fond partner who is fairly undemanding.

Passion, in other words, does not rage fearfully in your breast, though there is a chance that a non-sexual friendship up till now will become a more intimate one. But you may be in two minds about this.

If you bump into an old flame, you may have quite contradictory feelings. Pleased to be in touch, but fearful about letting it start up again.

January
Key Dates

Text in *italics* applies to everyone in the world.
Predictions in roman type apply to you alone.

Monday 1st: *An energetic start to the year, but there could be a romantic surprise. People are lively in small doses.* At home you could have clashes with a brother or sister. Daydreams will be fun, but are still a long way from reality.

Tuesday 2nd: *There's a vague start to the working year. Things get mislaid, people are unpunctual.* You will be called to judge something. Be fair rather than accurate! Good day for making money. A talk with a bank manager will be helpful.

Wednesday 3rd: *Still a vague, disillusioned time. Things may be done behind people's backs.* You're in the mood to let things slip. You don't care what others think. A shopping expedition will be successful.

Thursday 4th: *It's the start of an extravagant phase. People feel restless, looking for fun.* Not a sexy day, so your partner must find a good book. A social evening will enable you to make some new friends.

Friday 5th: *A day that's lucky for some, careless for others. Happiness will be short-lived.* Your career could move in a new direction, with beneficial results. You could feel a bit poorly, and will be slow on the uptake.

Saturday 6th: *Quite a gloomy weekend, when people feel down in the dumps. They may spend too much money.* You may be caught up in the law in some way. If you take part in a committee meeting, don't expect much co-operation.

Sunday 7th: *There could be sad headlines. People feel it's time they did something serious.* Kitchen equipment may be faulty. You have a special vitality today.

Monday 8th: *A realistic time, when things look a bit brighter. A way will be found out of difficulties.* If a new friendship beckons, make sure it isn't ruined before it starts.

Tuesday 9th: *Much more agile and lively, with plenty of fun to be had. People won't be solemn for long.* You are popular

38

among friends, and can even win an enemy over.

Wednesday 10th: *Sadly hopes are dashed. A day for tough negotiations, seeing things in a new light.* Someone you met last year could prove useful to you now. Follow a favourite jockey.

Thursday 11th: *Still a tough time, with delays likely. Not a good time for travel.* There will be changes at work, and you must stand up for your rights. At work a friend wants to move on to new places. Try to stay friends, even if you're moving apart.

Friday 12th: *A way is found out of difficulties. There's a new sense of co-operation.* Today should bring something special into your life.

Saturday 13th: *Quite a warm-hearted time, better for transport and travel. Lots of intuition in the air.* A parent will tell you some home truths. Romance could be wonderful this weekend, so long as you don't hide your feelings.

Sunday 14th: *A sensitive, carefree time when people don't want too much reality. A day of escapism and fantasy.* It's a good evening to go down memory lane, reliving the past. An irritable mood this morning gives way to an easy-going afternoon.

Monday 15th: *Still an unreal time, with people getting hold of the wrong end of the stick.* Little by little you get what you want. You may find your life restricted by the rule-book in some way.

Tuesday 16th: *The start of a warm-hearted phase when there's a nice air of jollity. Things won't be so bad.* You feel like giving someone a good ticking-off.

Wednesday 17th: *An excellent day for meeting someone new, starting up fresh friendships, and feeling lively.* Talk will be racy, and you may stupidly give a secret away.

Thursday 18th: *Very loving and co-operative day. It's much easier to relate to people – friends and foes alike.* Worry about practical problems shouldn't interfere with a good love life.

Friday 19th: *A day of adjustment and compromise. People change their minds to fit in with others.* A neighbour will be a good friend. You should pay a visit somewhere new.

Saturday 20th: *Still a friendly time, great for meeting new people and finding out happy surprises.* An unusual form of healing could works wonders for you.

Sunday 21st: *Another escapist weekend when no one wants to* *take life too seriously. A big emphasis on sexual love.* You must kiss goodbye to something that's meant a lot in the past.

Monday 22nd: *Lucky for some, a spending spree for others. People may push their luck.* You must turn your back on a situation that's no good. Look to your long- term happiness.

Tuesday 23rd: *Still a time to chance your arm, take risks and get away with it. Plenty of sexual happiness.* Friends may drop by, and arrange something for the weekend.

Wednesday 24th: *Life suits lots of people today. There's an air of success, and enjoying other people's company.* Visitors at home will bring a surprise present.

Thursday 25th: *Things seem happy-go-lucky, carefree and optimistic. A good day for success in business.* If you've been working hard, you should soon enjoy a triumph.

Friday 26th: *Very loving day, when agreement is reached and affection blossoms.* A group of you will have a splendid outing. Older friends aren't much help.

Saturday 27th: *A day of some surprise, with nothing quite certain. Doubts may be raised.* A child needs lots of company. Go out of your way to be helpful – schoolwork included.

Sunday 28th: *A super weekend for getting away from everything. But for some people there could be rows.* Be discreet if you discover something that's none of your business.

Monday 29th: *Romance could be exciting for some, dangerously unsettling for others. Don't believe all you hear.* Someone at work wants to see you out-of-hours.

Tuesday 30th: *People say one thing and mean another. They push their luck, and may not be very subtle.* If you are in love, you may be disappointed for a while.

Wednesday 31st: *A shock could catch people unawares. A day when things could go haywire.* Check your belongings, there's a hint that you might lose, drop, forget or mislay something.

Wise Words for January

Happiness is in the imagination.
What we perform is always inferior to what we imagine.
Cyril Connolly

February
Guide

Perhaps you're worried about something that may never happen. That's one aspect of life; in another you seem cock-a-hoop about developments, and will be busy making plans.

There is some tendency for people to take advantage of you, perhaps nicking your ideas or, worse still, your belongings. Do take special precautions against thieves this month.

Otherwise it seems a pleasant, if slightly low-spirited time for you. In the first week you plod along without anything much happening, but the second and third weeks are a bit depressing – not only in your own life but in other people's.

WORK. Your working days will be a bit slow and boring. You may be in the wrong job, of course, but now is not the right time to make a move. If an offer turns up, examine it carefully – especially if there's a risk involved – as it could all crumble to nothing in the next few months.

Another annoying factor will be a failure in communications. The phone or letter service could be on the blink, or people may be pretending not to have received information.

Better points to watch for: someone new in your work place makes you glad to be alive; a lick of paint or fresh equipment brightens up the place; and, if you're in management, you could get the thumbs up for a plan later in the year.

HOME. Most of the time will be happy enough, but you are all in a needling mood, critical of each other in the family. If you share a flat with friends, there could be some real arguments, and someone could walk out.

There could be signs of disrepair, especially in work that has only recently been completed. If you are thinking of renovating a kitchen or bathroom, you'll be inclined to make a good job of it – but this may mean waiting until you can afford it properly.

HEALTH. It's a month when you may want to freshen up

your looks with a new hairstyle, some fresh clothes and a slimming campaign. None of this will be easy, especially if you are feeling low-spirited.

It's important to attend to a minor health complaint before it gets worse. However trivial the symptoms, see the doctor and he may well have a treatment for it.

Don't ignore spiritual health, either. Stress can be the start of so many illnesses nowadays, and you must find some form of spiritual exercise – be it yoga, meditation or plain sleep.

MONEY. You may well be asked for money this month, so find out whether it's a good cause before giving. There is a suspicion that you could be involved in a confidence trick, making donations to an organisation that's crooked.

Thieving is definitely a possibility this month, so lock up carefully and make sure your insurance cover is up to date.

There will be one unexpected domestic expense – perhaps linked to another mouth to feed – and again you're going to have to hold back from a major purchase until later in the year.

LEISURE. Something old-fashioned and familiar will appeal to you, be it a Shakespearian play, an antique or a much-loved TV series. You aren't in the mood to change your ways.

It's not a wildly sociable month, and you may be staying clear of some people who have been troublesome. Perhaps you feel you're in someone's bad books, when this isn't the case at all – so it's better to stay in touch just to see how the land lies.

Watch out for: a special treat for someone who has been lonely or out of sorts recently; a love of drama and opera, and perhaps a visit to somewhere special; a new gadget or aid that makes the world of difference to a favourite pastime of yours; and improved TV, radio or hi-fi equipment in the household.

LOVE. There is a feeling that you are taking a friendship too much for granted, or being rather lazy in keeping it highly stimulated. Unless you make a bigger effort, your partner could be looking elsewhere.

If you feel you have been let down in the past, you will not easily forgive the person concerned. But this is a pity, as you are living in the past rather than looking forward to the future.

February
Key Dates

Text in *italics* applies to everyone in the world.
Predictions in roman type apply to you alone.

Thursday 1st: *Still a restless, rebellious time when people act impulsively.* Muscles will get tired if you work too hard. You're lucky with the colour yellow.

Friday 2nd: *People could be caught napping, just when they thought they were safe. A day of difficult decisions.* There could be a clash of principles with someone. You have a fine ability to bargain at the moment.

Saturday 3rd: *A depressing weekend for money, though there is a silver lining to the black cloud.* Have a spring clean on a room, cupboard, kitchen or car. You hate to be bullied by someone who's meant to be loving you.

Sunday 4th: *People could say cruel things to each other. A day of hard thinking, making sensible plans for the future.* Your health may not be good. A problem that's lain dormant for a while will start causing real pain.

Monday 5th: *A more relaxed time, but only briefly. The start of a difficult week at work.* There's good co-operation within the family circle. There could be a nice development in business.

Tuesday 6th: *Something's gotta give! There's a lot of pressure, which people may not stand up to.* You may have to repeat a job that you did earlier. Don't take a gamble unless you feel that the odds are really in your favour.

Wednesday 7th: *Still a tense, obsessive time for some people. There's bad news in the air.* Someone comes to you with a sob-story. You won't care as much as usual. These should be happy days for you, when no one is putting pressure on you.

Thursday 8th: *Nasty time, heralding problems in the week ahead. People are unreliable, and legal matters prove complicated.* You hear the inside story, which explains a lot. There's encouraging news about a young person you care about.

43

Friday 9th: *Depressing day for some people. Two terrible planetary aspects suggest bad news.* In your working day you get an unusual job which could lead to greater things.

Saturday 10th: *The ugly scene continues. People feel bloody-minded, without much kindness in their hearts.* You don't want to get too involved right now.

Sunday 11th: *A troubled weekend for many, with financial worries, loneliness or a lack of love.* They'll say one thing and do another, just when you thought you could rely on them.

Monday 12th: *People feel trapped, longing to break free. Agreements may be broken, and people act in an unpredictable way.* If you dither, you'll lose a promising opportunity. A daily chore will be made easier.

Tuesday 13th: *Things start to look better, but it is still a tense, no-holds-barred time.* Your plans could be obstructed. Patience is needed, but don't make too many compromises.

Wednesday 14th: *It may be Valentine's Day, but the Venus-Saturn conjunction makes it a bit gruelling.* There could be a touch of show business in your life. Someone else has bad luck, but you do much better.

Thursday 15th: *There's a brief pause between difficult aspects. An energetic time when things can be put in motion.* Cancer women are daring, and will force their menfolk out of a rut. The old will feel young again.

Friday 16th: *The end of a difficult working week, when people will be relieved to get away from problems.* You are quite psychic at the moment, and will pick up strange feelings.

Saturday 17th: *A weird weekend, when people's imaginations run riot. Energy could be misdirected.* If someone is really trying to sell you something, back off and think about it. Don't be talked into a decision straight away.

Sunday 18th: *No better, though it's lovely for artistic appreciation, or being swept off your feet by a new admirer!* You have lots of taste today in people, art and music.

Monday 19th: *Suddenly the sun bursts through! The week dawns bright, with luck, success and prosperity.* You may find yourself unable to help someone you like.

Tuesday 20th: *Things continue to look good, and people will heave a sigh of relief.* You must pull your socks up, with someone new around. You could even break the law, without realising it.

Wednesday 21st: *Quite pleasant, without any great dramas. Tempers have quietened down, and relationships seem better.* An idea of yours will be unfortunately taken up by someone else.

Thursday 22nd: *Plenty of fun, but a hard-working day when much can be achieved.* Don't be pushed around by an official.

Friday 23rd: *Wonderful day to clinch a deal, join a club, have a good time with others and achieve plenty.* In your personal life you will want to spend more time with a particular friend.

Saturday 24th: *Rather a bloody-minded day for some, when health may suffer and travel plans go awry.* You seem warm-hearted at the weekend, full of sensuality.

Sunday 25th: *An energetic weekend, and the start of a happier time for many. A sensual, sexy few days ahead.* You are quite cheerful, though a child will be difficult.

Monday 26th: *Plenty of warmth and colour in people's lives, with a liking for fun, flirting and frivolity.* Be thankful for small mercies. You won't get everything you want, but there's a compensation.

Tuesday 27th: *A somewhat surprising day or two, but still in an enjoyable mood. Some folk may be dulled into mistakes.* An extra pair of hands will make a big difference to your workload.

Wednesday 28th: *A sour note creeps in. There could be some cruelty or unfeeling action, spoiling the happiness.* Someone else's cooking may not agree with you.

Wise Words for February

Acquaintance: a degree of friendship called slight
when the object is poor or obscure,
and intimate when he is rich or famous.
Ambrose Bierce

45

March
Guide

The first ten days of March are a stop-go sort of time, when you make a good resolution only to break it, or find that a new development in your life is promptly contradicted.

But as March proceeds you become much more lively and good-humoured, and you may feel that a load is lifted from your shoulders. The turning point could be a jolly good row, or someone telling you some home truths. At all events, the air is cleared, a critical moment is passed.

As a typical Cancerian you like interfering in other people's lives, though you're always a bit fearful of doing so. This month is no exception, and you may stick your nose into someone's business just where it's not wanted.

WORK. There could be policy disagreements between you and management. You may feel that decisions from head office are wrong, or you are being put to a lot of trouble.

Apart from that, there is a lovely surprise coming your way, especially if you have been wanting to get closer to someone new at work. If you are thinking of making a move, this is a much better month to initiate proceedings; you are much more likely to find what you want.

HOME. A badly behaved teenager will be as good as gold for a while, and if you are young yourself with a difficult parent you will find life at home is easier from now on. This could be as a result of an almighty quarrel that makes things better.

Less happily, however, there could be a disagreement with another family in the neighbourhood. You may have to step in where angels fear to tread, trying to smooth a path on behalf of another member of the family – especially a young child.

Some Cancer people will be thinking of moving home soon. An opportunity may arise a little later in the year, but you should start making plans now.

HEALTH. A much healthier month than you have enjoyed recently, and even if you are chronically ill you should be feeling spry and in tip-top form from now on.

Cancer grown-ups are in danger of catching a childhood disease you failed to develop earlier on. It could be measles, mumps or chicken pox.

The other area that could create problems this month is your feet. You may need to visit a chiropodist, or perhaps there is something structural at fault.

MONEY. The influence suggesting lost money does continue during early March. Continue, therefore, to beware of losing cash through negligence or even theft.

Nevertheless the tide of fortune will soon be flowing in your direction again. The second half of March looks singularly lucky, when you could pick a winning streak in gambling and financial affairs generally.

If you enjoy investing in stocks and shares, there could be a new issue in an electronics or leisure firm that is widely tipped to burst past its offer price once it reaches market.

LEISURE. It's a good month to get in touch with old friends you haven't seen for years. If they get in touch with you, don't be grouchy and turn them down. Make an effort to see each other because it really will be a delightful experience.

Watch out for: the desire to make your garden extra-special this year, including a bit of structural change as well as spring colour; a surprising interest in someone else's hobby, which seems deadly dull to start with; the chance to sell something you've made, and to buy something beautiful with the proceeds; but, less happily, a tendency to drink more than usual – and for the drink to go to your head.

LOVE. If a partnership has gone through a dull patch recently, it will liven up towards the end of March. You get a strong wave of sexual charisma during this time, and not only will you feel attractive, but you will appear so to others.

As a result you could be attracting attention from new people, and one person in particular could take your fancy. Because you're not feeling wildly loyal and faithful at present, this could lead to a little flirtation on the side.

March
Key Dates

Text in *italics* applies to everyone in the world.
Predictions in roman type apply to you alone.

Thursday 1st: *Potentially a difficult day, with Mars and Saturn causing trouble. But there's light at the end of the tunnel.* Make a snap decision and you'll regret it later.

Friday 2nd: *Still a difficult time, with men behaving worse than women. There could be some deception in love.* Around the home there's a repair needing attention.

Saturday 3rd: *Excellent day for meeting people and enjoying group activities. There's a great sense of well-being.* Trouble with a sweetheart – you aren't on the same wavelength at all. Maybe it's better to stay out of each other's way.

Sunday 4th: *Marvellous weekend for travel, conversation, jokes and pleasure. People want to relax.* Nice day for a party.

Monday 5th: *Still a happy-go-lucky mood, with people meaning well and wanting to do their best.* You want to help others, but may not be up to it.

Tuesday 6th: *There's a strong gambling mood, which is also a bit slapdash and careless. A big decision is delayed.* A child may go too far, and you'll get angry.

Wednesday 7th: *The start of another difficult period in love. Money troubles could start to grow.* See something familiar in a new and interesting light.

Thursday 8th: *The ending of one chapter, and the beginning of a new one – but basically quite a favourable time.* Your ideas are getting bigger and bolder, especially where money is concerned. Perhaps you're planning to get rich quick!

Friday 9th: *The past can be put behind, and the future beckons. A lively, intelligent time for many.* As soon as you clear up, others will mess up! Lucky time: evening.

Saturday 10th: *It's a weekend when people must adapt to each other – or simply fall out.* Something nice may be organised behind your back.

Sunday 11th: *A quieter day, when people are confused. The*

48

desire to break free is overtaken by responsibility. Someone gets in touch – and you wished you'd been left alone.

Monday 12th: *A razzle-dazzle day when people feel dynamic and a bit bullying. They mean well, but the end result may not be very nice.* Love is in the air, but not in your heart. So others are frisky, while you say 'no'.

Tuesday 13th: *A calmer time, especially in business and practical affairs. Sensible decisions will be made.* If abroad, there could be a delay. Not nice for legal matters, either.

Wednesday 14th: *An excellent day for reaching agreements after long discussions. Things are moving ahead.* Concentrate on top priorities, don't get side-tracked.

Thursday 15th: *Quite a settled time in business, but romance is more jumpy and unexpected.* Your thoughts will be on a child's future. Be lucky with friends.

Friday 16th: *Still a slightly restless time for people who are looking for more independence.* A poorly neighbour will be more cheerful. A companion may not be very loving right now.

Saturday 17th: *A sensible day when older people get the better of the bargains. A good day for family affairs.* Good weekend for do-it-yourself activities.

Sunday 18th: *Quite a charming day, when people feel free to do what they want. A day for lazing about.* There could be home breakage today, so take care.

Monday 19th: *A lively, enterprising time when people are on the move and new possibilities are discussed.* You seem nervous – perhaps worried about a coming event. You need a comforting chat with someone wise and experienced.

Tuesday 20th: *Still a chattering time, when people may say one thing and do another – or not do it at all.* A difficult day. There may be a hard choice to make. A bargain will be good value.

Wednesday 21st: *Another easy-going day with the accent on travel, fun and adventure.* The health of some Cancerians won't be too hot at the moment. There's a big show of loyalty.

Thursday 22nd: *Another happy-go-lucky day, with lots of affection within the family.* You may be introduced to someone new: dark and silent to start with.

Friday 23rd: *People feel extravagant, whether or not they've got* *the money! There's a note of danger, though.* There could be a row in front of others. You will benefit with someone else's tips. Your own intuition isn't too good.

Saturday 24th: *A weekend when things may change in romance. Some people are very firm-minded.* If you are normally a shy type, this is the time to cast modesty aside.

Sunday 25th: *A lively, strong-minded day when people are not inclined to forgive and forget.* A sweetheart could go off you for a while, but come round to your way of thinking.

Monday 26th: *There could be a sudden moment of success for some people, or a narrow squeak for others.* Life may have been boring recently, but better times are ahead.

Tuesday 27th: *Rather a vague, indeterminate day. Lies may be told, and people may not admit the truth.* Face up to a situation you have been trying to ignore.

Wednesday 28th: *Quite pleasant, with people looking for fun. This could be a winning day for many.* Be neighbourly, and invite someone old or helpless out for a treat.

Thursday 29th: *There could be some stormy relationships, and rows within a group of people. Some get bullied!* A competitive day when you really want to win. Don't be fobbed off with second-best.

Friday 30th: *Another tempestuous day when the unexpected can easily occur.* You're a desirable person in lots of ways. Unfortunately the wrong person will get the wrong idea.

Saturday 31st: *Another lively, jumpy time when people don't know whether they're coming or going.* Don't get snarled up with the law, or things will go badly for you.

Wise Words for March

Action springs not from thought,
but from a readiness for responsibility.
Dietrich Bonhoeffer

April
Guide

You remain good-humoured and happy for much of the month, even though there may be one or two problems.

One person in particular may be a trouble to you, saying one thing but doing another. There could be delays as a result, and you will wonder whether you are getting anywhere. Leaving that aside, you may also have to commit yourself to a tiresome duty. Although you may be dreading this, it will actually work out better than expected.

Quite apart from your own attitude, life will start to become more exciting this April. One or two new opportunities will be opening up, and you feel strongly in the mood to take advantage of them. Obviously it depends how entrepreneurial you are, but if you are the business type you could snap up an exciting work opportunity – and if you're the flirty, sexy type there could certainly be someone new to hold!

WORK. Many Cancer people will be turning a new business idea over in your mind. Even if you don't normally work for a living, there could be a new part-time possibility.

If you run your own business, things look very rosy. Several new opportunities will come your way, and with one you could make a lot of money quickly.

In a more ordinary nine-till-five occupation there could be one change in your working routine that you dislike. It could involve unsocial hours, or the withdrawal of a facility.

HOME. Things seem very happy at home. A relative who often leans on you will start becoming much more independent, and a child who has been a disappointment in the past is now well able to take care of themselves.

Every Cancerian loves home life, and this month more than most. You will enjoy entertaining at home, freshening-up the garden, doing a touch of redecoration and generally feeling very pleased with yourself. If a change of house is indicated, it's most likely to be taking place within the next month or two.

HEALTH. There could be a minor eruption on the skin: a stye, a wart, a boil – that sort of thing.

If you have recently been given a disappointing diagnosis, the news this month will be better. It is well worth while taking a second opinion, and new tests may reveal your condition to be less worse than feared.

MONEY. You could be making an important binding agreement at this time: a contract, an agreement, a commitment to pay money for quite a while.

You may be under pressure to spend quite a lot, whether you have it or not. Cancer people will be running into debts at this time, but you're confident that you will recoup these losses.

LEISURE. Some of your leisure time will be taken up with a responsibility you would prefer someone else to tackle. But once you get your teeth into it, it will be quite a tasty morsel, and you feel that you learn from the experience.

What's more, at some stage this month you can learn through the mistakes of others, especially in sport or some other competitive hobby. With the change of seasons imminent, you could well be taking up a new sport or outdoor activity and plunging enthusiastically into the learning process.

Watch out for: several nice evenings out, though they may cost plenty; the chance to support your home team in a worth while cause; a nice break, if only for several days, which involves educational culture; an a new neighbour who proves surprisingly congenial.

LOVE. Some Cancer people will feel that their sweetheart is deceiving them, or you may simply not feel very settled and happy about the relationship. Everything may seem fine on the surface, but underneath you are a bit worried.

Perhaps in any romance you are feeling a bit stand-offish at present, not wanting to be taken for granted. For other Cancer people there will be the opportunity to start a brand-new romance, which does make you put an existing relationship into the shade. You just can't help your own feelings.

Best links are with Leo and Sagittarius.

April
Key Dates

Text in *italics* applies to everyone in the world.
Predictions in roman type apply to you alone.

Sunday 1st: *One or two puzzles, with no clear-cut answers. Quite a pleasant day, but a mystery in romance.* A hard-up day. You could be locked out or caught out.

Monday 2nd: *Pleasant and lively, with the accent on social life. This could be the start of a successful week for many.* There could be some sad news, but it won't get you down.

Tuesday 3rd: *Ideal for getting together with others, reaching agreement and making joint plans.* There could be trouble with a pet. You must pay overdue bills, or there'll be real trouble.

Wednesday 4th: *Slightly muddled time, though people mean well on the whole. Lots of drive to achieve plenty.* There could be a spot of romance in the daylight hours.

Thursday 5th: *An amiable day for some, a hard-working time for others. Victory could slip out of the grasp.* In the right social setting, you'll find that you are popular.

Friday 6th: *Ideal for travel, adventure, getting away from it all. Money could go missing.* You want to feel on top of the world, but someone's dragging you down.

Saturday 7th: *A turning-point for some, but mainly a happy weekend when people seem cheerful.* If travelling, beware of short cuts. There is a chance to shine in company.

Sunday 8th: *Some people come up against a brick wall, but for most it's a relaxed, jolly weekend.* You can have a real giggle with your best friend. Have fun with a sweetheart too, though voices may get heated on one particular issue.

Monday 9th: *A super start to the week, with real love in the air. People want to have a good time.* Sports enthusiasts will have a terrific day. Be lucky with the colour green.

Tuesday 10th: *Very lively, quick-witted and romantic time, with the emphasis on spending money.* You think you know the answer to everything! A small injury or blemish will hurt your pride more than your looks.

Wednesday 11th: *An intelligent day when success is likely. An easy spell for many.* A surprise could leave you tongue-tied. You're in a creative mood, so start designing!

Thursday 12th: *Still amiable and loving, though someone could be pulling the wool over your eyes.* A child may go too far, and you'll get angry. A friend will go on whining.

Friday 13th: *For once this date could bring some bad luck, with Mars contacting Saturn and Uranus.* Sexually you should feel happier, more lively and vivacious.

Saturday 14th: *People are still slightly at odds with each other, and a difference turns into an all-out row.* Love is all the sweeter if you've been kept apart. Be ready to travel far for love's sake!

Sunday 15th: *Sunshine and showers today, with some nice news in romance and money.* Hold on to a possession rather than give it to the wrong person.

Monday 16th: *Still some aggro in the air, but most people will comfortably be able to forget it.* An average day when life seems fairly easy. There could be some trouble in your street.

Tuesday 17th: *A great time for making plans, dreaming dreams and being creative.* You'll full of enthusiasm, but that won't get the job done. You need the help of others, however much you want to do things on your own.

Wednesday 18th: *Things could come to a full stop because of difficulties. A hoped-for development may be cancelled.* You stay cheerful, but other people will drag you down.

Thursday 19th: *Disruptions in travel, plans getting cancelled, a lot of hard thinking.* While the cat's away, you can play! Somehow in your life the barriers will drop and you'll let rip.

Friday 20th: *People feel under pressure, particularly to do with career. Nice for romance and the arts.* A sexy mood can quickly turn to spite if you feel you aren't getting enough attention.

Saturday 21st: *For some people there's a problem you can't get out of your mind.* Home life is pleasant. One of your good days.

Sunday 22nd: *Problems have a good chance of easing away,* *or at least people feel a corner has been turned.* You want to spend on yourself, not others. A decision of yours will meet with general approval.

Monday 23rd: *Excellent for romance or money, especially if a momentous decision has been made.* A jolly day among friends. On your own you'll feel downcast.

Tuesday 24th: *Some people will be acting stupidly, but most will still feel under mental pressure.* There could be a slight improvement at work.

Wednesday 25th: *Quite an explosive time, when there could be a disaster in the news.* Someone is hiding something from you – but it will do harm to find out more.

Thursday 26th: *Slightly luckier, but tempers can explode on the least pretext.* Make a big effort to tidy up a mess, whether it's a scruffy home or a love life in ruins!

Friday 27th: *Every reason to remain optimistic, even though some people are a pain in the neck.* It's another warmly relaxing day for most Cancerians. Go off somewhere new.

Saturday 28th: *There are threats in the air, and people are a bit accident-prone.* Your heart is full of love, so be generous and share it out!

Sunday 29th: *Great for sport, travel and adventure, but still not a peaceful environment.* There could be one blemish in your good looks – do what you can, but don't be too self-conscious.

Monday 30th: *Surprises continue. It's a good day for wriggling out of problems.* Children need help to start with, then they are fine on their own.

Wise Words for April

In matters of art it is more blessed
to respond than to judge.
David Cecil

May
Guide

May seems an exciting time when the opportunities that may have arisen last month start coming to fruition.

There could be several surprises, including an invitation out of the blue, but for many Cancer people an idle dream in the past could become present reality.

Life really seems to be moving forward on several fronts. At its most dramatic, you could be starting a new job, moving home or making a major change in a relationship. Less vividly perhaps, you will simply feel nicely buoyant, riding on a gentle crest of the wave when all seems for the best.

WORK. Learning something new at work won't be easy, but well worth while in the end. You may finally master something you have only half-understood up till now, and so Cancer students revising for exams are likely to get their act together.

It's an ideal time to be doing well at an interview and being offered a job. If there has been a history of past failures, you may suddenly get your career right at long last!

You will want to spread your wings, which is why a move of house could well be indicated around mid-1990. It's a great time for getting work experience abroad, or working for a multi-national company.

HOME. This seems a sociable time, perhaps with visitors calling. It could be a melting-pot time too, when you are plunged into the deep end in some way. Cancer mums who have just had a new child – especially a first one – will really feel the presence of the young one.

This is the most likely month for a change of house, and although you always disliked this kind of change, you will settle in better than normal. The new neighbourhood may seem alarming at first, but will actually be quite welcoming.

HEALTH. There are no indications of big problems on the health front. You should be bonny and bright, and if you are manic-depressive at the best of times this is certainly going to be one of your manic times!

What's more, you seem to have a cheerful healing quality for those around you. You can lift other people's spirits, and, whether you realise it or not, you seem to have a gift of spiritual healing that can be wonderful.

MONEY. You could be out of pocket due to someone else's mistake. You have to pay for the consequences, or contribute more than your fair share.

It's a good time for getting a pay rise or an improved salary if you move elsewhere. If you run your own business, profits should be looking bright around now.

You will enjoy shopping, especially for something you've never bought before. Although you may take expert advice, in the end you will buy according to your instincts.

LEISURE. In your leisure hours it seems a snug, lazy time when you won't want to tackle too much. You feel like getting up late, pottering about, and not exerting yourself too much.

You are very keen on mixed company, and will enjoy giving a party where you can bring disparate friends together and see how everyone gets on.

Watch out for: the chance to meet someone famous, if only briefly; a delight in a pageant, celebration or special public occasion; and becoming a friend of someone else's kids, though they may not like their own parents very much.

LOVE. There's a lot of hot passion in your life, if only you could give vent to it. Some Cancer people will be sex-mad at present, so it could be a really exciting, if short-lived, time.

I'm not saying that this will necessarily be with your nearest and dearest. There's more of a suggestion of a mad, passionate fling with someone else – so hot and bothered, in fact, that you know it can't last long.

For some Cancer people, of course, this will only be an infatuation. It never gets past the looking-and-longing stage. For others, especially if you've recently wed, it will be within a long-standing partnership.

May
Key Dates

**Text in *italics* applies to everyone in the world.
Predictions in roman type apply to you alone.**

Tuesday 1st: *An intriguing day when one problem gets solved and a new one arises.* You're full of ideals, but they aren't very practical at the moment.

Wednesday 2nd: *A subtle, intuitive time when insights are likely. People may be argumentative.* A grown-up child may be taking the wrong route – but don't interfere.

Thursday 3rd: *A disagreeing time, but not a disagreeable one. People are inclined to let things coast.* An entertaining day. You need to be out and about, meeting people.

Friday 4th: *Much brighter and on the ball, with plenty of new ideas brewing.* Work will be a challenge. There may be a new face to welcome – or welcome back?

Saturday 5th: *A lovely weekend for lazing, strolling and not making too much effort.* Don't take risks with electricity. You could win at the races with a careful examination of form.

Sunday 6th: *Still a laid-back time, with people inclined to have a good time.* Ideal weekend to get away from it all. You may feel you're taken advantage of.

Monday 7th: *A slightly more meaningful day when something hidden comes to light.* A lovely day. You have plenty of self-confidence. Time to keep children busy. You must teach a youngster to be more modest.

Tuesday 8th: *Still a potentially explosive time in some areas, with squabbles likely.* You will enjoy a group leisure activity. There is now a question-mark over a planned holiday.

Wednesday 9th: *It looks a bright, inventive time when people are full of resourcefulness.* There could be some cheating you do not approve of. You receive a valuable tip, perhaps from someone you love.

Thursday 10th: *Lively and versatile, but there could be a narrow squeak, especially in a dangerous situation.* You need to get outside. If training, you'll do really well.

Friday 11th: *Broadly a nice, easy-going day, when some people could be lucky*. If you're not on holiday, it's an ideal time to be planning your next break. Get the brochures out!

Saturday 12th: *Very much a resourceful weekend when victory could come from nowhere*. Jolly day, good for telepathy with others. No good chasing after a lost cause.

Sunday 13th: *A great time for having fun. Unexpected friendships will blossom*. If you're too shy, you'll get nowhere. Some problems from an in-law.

Monday 14th: *Excellent for travel, fun, exploration and making the best of a bad job!* You're very conscious of your effect on others, for better or worse. A self-aware day.

Tuesday 15th: *Still a lucky time, when a fantastic surprise could turn up*. Good day for making business contacts. Nice romantic date, especially if you haven't seen each other for a while.

Wednesday 16th: *Slightly more settled, but people may seek freedom instead of responsibility*. A day of varying moods. One moment you'll be sensitive, the next loud-mouthed.

Thursday 17th: *A good time to reach agreement and make long-term decisions. A lucky time*. People are slipshod. You can't settle to anything. There may be an underlying worry.

Friday 18th: *People should enjoy themselves, but perhaps at the expense of others*. Plenty of fun and high spirits. You feel fit and well, and will be trying to exercise at home – perhaps jogging with the family?

Saturday 19th: *A day when people may seal their fate, without quite realising what they are doing*. Someone may be prying into your affairs, without your knowing it. Luckily you're in a confident mood.

Sunday 20th: *Again a bright-eyed, bushy-tailed time when people are on the go*. There could be problems in the garden – damage, vandalism, pests?

Monday 21st: *Still lucky and sunny for many people, with no real disasters in the air*. A happy day, especially if you can get right away from day-to-day concerns.

Tuesday 22nd: *Lots of fun, with people good-humoured and seeking agreement*. You feel close to someone, but may still

59

have to keep a secret from them.

Wednesday 23rd: *Another lovely day with plenty of good things happening. People can't help feeling romantic!* Make the most of people who love you. Don't start an argument, as you could destroy their affection.

Thursday 24th: *Excellent time for striving hard with a particular aim in view. The luck continues.* You're scared to follow your own judgment. Some help as far as a financial problem is concerned.

Friday 25th: *Mild arguments breaking out, but they're not important. Most people should feel happy.* There may be a legal problem threatening. Be careful on the roads.

Saturday 26th: *Slightly grim for some people, with a disappointment possible.* You bump into someone who's really changed since you last met.

Sunday 27th: *Nice for travel, going places, feeling a sudden rush of desire.* Do something different. Don't pine after someone who can't be with you.

Monday 28th: *Still a bonny time, with people wanting to forget their troubles. Excellent for travel.* A small effort makes a big difference. Some government news could help you.

Tuesday 29th: *Quite sexy, but with hostilities breaking out if people get upset or jealous.* An evening out is fun.

Wednesday 30th: *A blissful day or two if you have no problems. You may be living in cloud-cuckoo land.* People give you all sorts of conflicting advice.

Thursday 31st: *Quite warm-hearted but some people won't co-operate with a well-laid plan.* Plans go through without a murmur. You handle a complicated situation with grace.

Wise Words for May

Beauty is an experience, nothing else.
It is not a fixed pattern or an arrangement of features.
It is something *felt*.

D.H. Lawrence

June
Guide

June continues the good work of May. You should feel that you are still riding a high, and what's more there could be a surprise bonus – in love as much as anything else.

But things aren't all lovey-dovey. You may witness something unpleasant – perhaps nothing directly to do with your own life, but which you may have to report to the police. Alternatively it could be the sight of two friends rowing.

You do seem to be in the public eye in some way. You might get a record request aired at long last, or take part in a phone-in programme, or be giving a little talk to a local club.

WORK. Broadly speaking your sweet-natured personality does well at the work scene. You are particularly effective in work that calls for charm and allure, whether you are a hostess, a social worker, a receptionist or whatever.

But you do get a come-uppance in something. Perhaps you've been taking something too much for granted, and then suddenly find you are being tested in a different way. This may be a shock if you are taking exams, because however hard you may have revised, there will be surprise questions.

But you could get bogged down in paperwork and officialdom at this stage of the year, and find yourself wasting days on tax problems, planning permission or whatever.

HOME. Family influence makes itself felt this month. If you were planning to go ahead without family permission, forget it – even if you don't really need it, you'll feel guilty without it.

You could have quite a spring-cleaning, but throw out something which later you find you need. But you will feel all the better for a good clear-out.

There could be a clash between home duties and leisure hours. Baby-sitting, for instance, could prevent you from having as much fun as you would like, and if you employ anyone around the home, there could be growing tension.

HEALTH. If last month was lazy, June looks more active. You will enjoy some extra exercise, perhaps due to the influence of a visitor or a new friend in your life.

One problem could occur when you are barefoot, especially around a beach. Make sure that you have a tetanus jab in good time, or a cut in the garden could prove nasty.

MONEY. You seem in an egging-on mood when you want to urge others to spend, even if you can't yourself. You may be helping someone to buy clothes for a trousseau, furniture for a new home or equipment for a brand-new business.

You seem in quite a generous mood yourself, and, as I say, there could be a surprise bonus this month: money that you didn't expect to receive. Obviously this could be a little pools win, or a nice little run of winners at the races.

LEISURE. You may feel let down by a friend, but there's no need – if you brood about it, nothing gets better, but if you forgive and forget you will soon be friends again.

You are in quite a possessive mood, and will rather hoard your belongings. Although you may throw some things away, you are busy accumulating others.

You will enjoy the long summer evenings, especially if you live near water. You seem to be making more journeys than usual this month, and although most of them will be pleasant, one will be a complete waste of time.

Watch out for: a child with nothing to do; a grown-up who interferes too much; a party that gets too rough for your liking; and an unusual entertainment that really appeals.

LOVE. If you feel you have been neglected in the recent past, you could become quite irritable. But the likelihood is that one blessing will be piled upon another.

If last month was sex-mad, the passionate phase does continue into June – certainly the first half. Some lucky single Cancerians will have not just one marvellous love affair but perhaps several. You still have plenty of sexual charisma.

This applies whether you normally are a heart-throb or not. Even a Cancer person who has been out of romantic action for some time will find it much easier to attract people.

June
Key Dates

**Text in *italics* applies to everyone in the world.
Predictions in roman type apply to you alone.**

Friday 1st: *A grand day for reaching agreement with others. There will be smiles and handshakes.* You'll set several balls rolling. Fair day for gambling. You could be lucky with a raffle.

Saturday 2nd: *A great time to join with others – whether it's a club outing or a happy family occasion.* An overseas holiday is on your mind. Whatever your heart says, your head will keep your plans practical.

Sunday 3rd: *An everyday day, without any great dramas. People are trusting to luck.* You will be involved in someone else's romantic troubles. Follow family wishes. Don't be a tyrant among people you love.

Monday 4th: *A larky, sparky sort of day when things go well. Definitely an air of good fortune.* Enjoy yourself, but don't tease someone who can't take it – or it will end in tears.

Tuesday 5th: *Things aren't being worked out very carefully. There could be surprises in store.* Everyone's busy except yourself. If you have a touchy partner, tread carefully.

Wednesday 6th: *A lucky time for many, and there could be an unexpected winner in the Derby.* You have to pick the lesser of two evils. A gamble you've often made in the past could work out well now. Favourite numbers could win – at last.

Thursday 7th: *Still a day of surprises, with lots of happy encounters for people.* You can bounce out of a depression. There's an important decision to make concerning a child. You must follow your judgment, but please others.

Friday 8th: *A more cautious day, good for signing legal documents and doing serious business.* More happiness. You should feel on top of the world.

Saturday 9th: *The luck runs out for some people. Quite a sexy day for others, especially in chance encounters.* A very lively approach to life. You'll be a success at work, especially if things don't go according to plan.

Sunday 10th: *Another lucky period begins, especially if you are striving for success.* There could be some ill-health, especially a stomach complaint.

Monday 11th: *A happy time in love, when you just want to live in a world of fantasy.* If you're active in politics, you run up against some problems. But you'll thrive on all the activity!

Tuesday 12th: *A lucky day, especially if you follow your intuition. An important day in love lives everywhere.* Nice romantic date, especially if you haven't seen each other for a while.

Wednesday 13th: *Still a crucial make-or-break day for some people, but you should end up smiling.* You'll have to say goodbye to a treasured possession.

Thursday 14th: *Basically a successful time, especially in group efforts. The tide flows in your favour.* Good day at work. You get help with a nasty task.

Friday 15th: *A nice day for some, but there could be a momentary disappointment over something you were counting on.* Beware of seeming too vain. A steady weekend. You'll get plenty done, and can learn much through coaching, talks, etc.

Saturday 16th: *A slightly down-beat weekend when you may feel gloomy for no good reason. Things don't quite work out.* There will be a slightly downbeat mood to the day.

Sunday 17th: *Again a time of some discord and niggling, with nothing quite fitting together.* Not a brilliant time for love-making. There could be a lack of response.

Monday 18th: *Much better, with quarrels forgotten and a happier mood all round. There are strong, passionate feelings.* Quite a sporting day. You're prepared to have a go, and never mind the consequences.

Tuesday 19th: *On the whole a better mood, with common sense prevailing over rash passion.* It doesn't seem as if you've learnt the lesson. You're going over the top again.

Wednesday 20th: *Still a steady time, when older people do better than younger ones. There could be some drama.* Keep things steady. There could be a lot on your plate, so plod on.

Thursday 21st: *You may feel a milestone has been passed.*

There is good sense being talked. Some extra cash comes in handy. You're in an extravagant mood.

Friday 22nd: *Nothing very special indicated, though travel seems favoured as well as a few friendly arguments!* There could be a touch of glamour, all the same.

Saturday 23rd: *Another easy-going day when nothing is taken too seriously. There's an emphasis on romance.* Very friendly and affectionate. You're good at starting up a friendship.

Sunday 24th: *A warm-hearted, lively time when people are inclined to push their luck.* Forgetful day. Keep a list if it helps.

Monday 25th: *Quite a happy time, though there's a note of bullying in the air.* More love and hate in the family circle! Some relative seems stirred up and angry.

Tuesday 26th: *A bit rash and impulsive, but not seriously so. No very important planetary aspects today.* An escapist mood. You can't concentrate on your work.

Wednesday 27th: *A good day for talks about financial problems, perhaps dealing with the long-term future.* Not one of your easiest days. Restrain others from excessive spending.

Thursday 28th: *Another reasonable day when nobody wants to make too great an effort.* Your health could be slightly delicate. Excellent weekend for being away from home.

Friday 29th: *A day when you can create surprises around you, or have a surprise sprung on you – all for the best.* One of your clever-clever days when you think you're the brightest person in the world.

Saturday 30th: *Another surprising day, when you mustn't be too rash and impulsive.* Pleasant day. If buying equipment, be very practical and compare prices.

Wise Words for June

A business that makes nothing but money
is a poor kind of business.
Henry Ford

July
Guide

At some stage this month you'll get just the right help – and just when you need it. So don't despair. If you feel you are in a fix, a shining knight may come along on a white charger.

This doesn't mean that everything is going to go well. There could certainly be one disappointment, with a delay or cancellation likely. You may have to put up with something out-of-date for a while longer.

For the first part of July you feel in quite a mischievous mood, and may enjoy teasing someone. If they tease you in return, you'll be furious!

In the second half of July it's best to make a clean breast of a worry close to your heart. You may be bottling up problems that won't seem nearly so bad once they've been discussed.

WORK. You seem in a hesitant mood, especially where a job change is concerned. If unemployed and looking for work, you could be offered something – but by hesitating you could lose it.

Some Cancer people will have a brand new business opportunity presented to them on a plate and it's the same story – too much caution, not enough bravery.

You may get obsessed with a certain idea, and can't get it out of your mind. This could be economic security, long-term loyalty to an existing boss, or a feeling that every job should be done perfectly – or you won't be satisfied.

HOME. There could be one or two mini-disasters at home: nothing serious, you understand, and they may actually work out to your advantage. If something gets broken, for instance, you will be secretly pleased.

One member of the family will get on your nerves, especially if you feel that he or she is not making enough effort. You won't be seeing so much of one relative for a while, and although you're anxious you know it's the right move.

If you leave home yourself this month, you'll be delighted at the beginning but then become homesick. But these are only teething problems, and you'll soon be happy with your new life.

HEALTH. There could be something wrong with a joint or muscle that gives some background pain. A twisted ankle won't heal itself quickly enough.

If you have any mental disorder you'll be pleased how well you are coping now. If you have been confused or anxious, life seems much calmer from now on.

There could be some dental work necessary around now, but less than perhaps you feared.

MONEY. Shopping will be good fun, especially in the sales. You can stock up on a number of items that have got old or outworn: towels, cutlery, even a carpet.

On the credit side you could do well in a competition, especially one calling for a little skill. If you have a disappointment in gambling, it could quickly be followed by a run of luck.

LEISURE. This is an excellent month for setting out on a journey, whether it's an annual holiday or something more permanent. You'll enjoy going anywhere new, but a visit to a familiar place will seem rather boring.

Certainly you deserve a relaxing month after quite a few weeks of ups and downs. You're in a party mood, and there could be a couple of invitations that catch your fancy.

Watch out for: a friend of a friend who makes a pass; trouble at a weekend, eating into your leisure time; another weekend when you get help just at the right time; and a visit in company, especially to do with music, which appeals to your imagination.

LOVE. This is quite a loving month, especially within a fond, long-term relationship like marriage.

But you must be true to your own feelings. You aren't good at dissembling, faking passion or trying to go along with someone else's image of yourself.

If you are looking for someone new, there could be links with someone who is already attached elsewhere. Some Cancer people will pinch a sweetheart off their best friend.

But it's not a wildly sensual month.

July
Key Dates

Text in *italics* applies to everyone in the world.
Predictions in roman type apply to you alone.

Sunday 1st: *A madcap day when people do crazy things! Quite fun, but there could be a touch of danger, too.* Fix a repair promptly, and be busy in the garden.

Monday 2nd: *A lively, quick-witted day, and quite sexy too. People should feel on the ball, ready for anything.* You could lose something in the course of your daily work. A romance at work should advance by leaps and bounds.

Tuesday 3rd: *Another bright-as-a-button day, but there could be some tough negotiations as well.* You're also in the mood to criticise others, which won't be appreciated.

Wednesday 4th: *Hopes are dashed, and people lose concentration. A good idea becomes fuzzy at the edges.* An older relative needs special help at this time.

Thursday 5th: *Things could go awry, plans get spoilt, but in the end agreement can be reached.* Someone on the telly could arouse your righteous indignation.

Friday 6th: *Another tender, vulnerable day when people could be conned – or let themselves in for more trouble.* Someone could be kicked out, for no good reason.

Saturday 7th: *A more realistic time, terrific for travel and adventure. Taking a risk will be well worth while.* If you have a form to fill in, you'll be flummoxed!

Sunday 8th: *Another airy, free-and-easy day, but there are snags. First the sunshine, then the showers!* Not a lucky weekend, but a persevering one. Your health may be slightly below-par, so don't burn the candle at both ends.

Monday 9th: *Quite a loving time, with the emphasis on sweethearts and small children!* At work you could be moved to a new department. Lucky time: early afternoon.

Tuesday 10th: *There's some melancholy in the air, as though people can't have quite what they want.* You are worried about your standard of living, and must give something up.

Wednesday 11th: *Anger is in the air. People may be rash, speaking out of turn, and hopes could be dashed.* A business venture may run into troubles, and someone could be planning to interfere in your affairs.

Thursday 12th: *There is a silver lining, but the clouds look awfully black! It's still a day of rows.* In your working day you must tell a white lie to avoid a fuss.

Friday 13th: *First the good news, then the bad news. A difficult day to do with the law, travel, education.* You'll bump into some old friends and perhaps meet some new ones, too.

Saturday 14th: *Lucky for some, disappointing for others. Victory is close, but success may still be missed.* Your partner has a change of mind, which throws you in a tizzy.

Sunday 15th: *Quite pleasant and lucky, though there could be a background worry. Not an easy time.* Pet animals can be too much of a good thing. The family should be strong and healthy.

Monday 16th: *Now the luck seems to triumph over ill-luck. Disappointments fade, while hopes rise.* You may regret a risky thing you did a while ago.

Tuesday 17th: *It remains a happy, positive and ambitious time when there's plenty for most people to look forward to.* You'll be in a restless mood, and will hate being cooped up.

Wednesday 18th: *People need to be talked out of a mood or won over with compliments. There's plenty of anger in the air.* Get a move on if you want to sign up for a leisure activity.

Thursday 19th: *Slightly mixed-up day when plans don't always work out. A gathering could be spoilt by bad behaviour.* Life with your partner is a bit fraught at present. You'll feel you're being taken advantage of.

Friday 20th: *Another slightly edgy day when some people are more obstinate than ever.* Don't tolerate slap-happy attitudes at work. You should be reaping the benefit of good work.

Saturday 21st: *A bit better, with smiles instead of frowns. People feel lucky, but could be on a wild goose-chase.* There will be progress, and considerable changes should take place.

Sunday 22nd: *An energetic day, but tempers could flare without warning. Good for taking sensible risks.* There's a small item to fix at home, making the place look prettier.

Monday 23rd: *A day when surprises could flash out of the blue, and carelessness could triumph.* A young friend gives happiness. One lie will lead to another.

Tuesday 24th: *A day of small niggles and disappointments, but nothing too serious. There's a lack of co-operation.* You'll be at odds with a lover: friendly one moment, fighting the next.

Wednesday 25th: *Surprises and upsets are likely, but on the credit side there could be extra money coming.* There's a further change in your working routine – probably for the worse. Luckily it won't last long.

Thursday 26th: *Still a lively, unpredictable time, especially as far as finance or romance are concerned.* Give advice to youngsters, but avoid repeating yourself.

Friday 27th: *A bit calmer, with nobody wanting to rock the boat too much. There could be a disappointment.* Workmen will be helpful. You will be asked for money, so find out whether it's a good cause before giving.

Saturday 28th: *The start of a sexy weekend, with lots of warm-hearted behaviour. Great for starting a holiday!* In negotiations you may realize that your trump cards aren't too good, after all.

Sunday 29th: *Still a happy and sensitive time, when people need a change of routine, with plenty of extra stimulation.* Don't turn down an invitation. It may not be much in itself, but it could lead to greater things.

Monday 30th: *Great for romance and creativity, but you could be deceived by appearances. Not a realistic time.* If you're courting, you won't have much time to yourselves.

Tuesday 31st: *Not a good day for family affairs, as people seem at sixes and sevens.* A child may give you a scary moment, but all ends well.

Wise Words for July

Chaos often breeds life,
when order breeds habit.
Henry Brooks Adams

August
Guide

This seems a sunshine-and-showers sort of month, when you may give a lot of joy to others just to forget your own troubles.

I don't mean that there will be anything seriously wrong with your life, but there could be a couple of problems.

One may be quite specific and practical, dealing with career or finance in particular. The other could be a vague unease in the background of your mind.

Every Cancer person can be bluff and courageous on the outside, but inside is a squirming mass of nerves! This is particularly apparent this August, when everyone will think you are throwing your weight around – but really you are much more circumspect and shy.

WORK. In some ways you could be trying too hard, and earn a reprimand. Other people, particularly fellow-workers, may want you to toe the line, but you're too ambitious for that.

If you are expecting exam results, they could be more gratifying than you ever guessed. You may have to revise your plans upward as far as further education is concerned.

Accounts and calculations could be faulty, and need to be done again. You could certainly spend part of your working month searching for one small fault that is spoiling everything.

HOME. If you are feeling homesick or dissatisfied with your present surroundings, open your eyes and you may suddenly see them in a more attractive light. It could be caused by a nice neighbour you discover, or simply a feeling that you're getting used to your new environment.

Even in an old familiar home, you may see it through fresh eyes. A little extra decoration, or a new purchase for the living room, could make just the difference. If you've great plans for the garden, so much the better.

Perhaps you are worried about a child who is refusing to grow up, or one that is growing up all too fast!

HEALTH. Soon you're going to have to spend money on your health. It could be something you cannot get under your health insurance or the NHS, so it could be something non-essential and perhaps unorthodox. You might decide to try an alternative treatment that someone has recommended, or you might be going on a special training course to practice healing yourself. It's a great time to be learning more on an out-of-the-way subject so that you can be more healthy yourself.

MONEY. Your financial affairs could be getting out of control, and you are going to have to devise a new plan to get them back on the straight and narrow. This could involve a formal loan from a bank or building society, with proper repayments. You may decide to use a direct-debit scheme, or one of the new smart cards in your favourite supermarket.

So it's a good month for switching funds from one investment to another. You may be thinking about a personal pension plan, whether you are self-employed or not.

LEISURE. New friends could make a big difference on your outlook on life. They may be somewhat different from yourself, and cheer you up enormously.

Someone could get the wrong idea about you, with embarrassing results. They may think that you are more brash and aggressive than you really are. But certainly you are tackling your leisure life hammer and tongs this August.

Watch out for: getting help and advice from an expert in a favourite hobby; having an alarming journey in unusual circumstances; vowing to collect something after a visit to a museum; and enjoying the simple pleasures of summer life.

LOVE. One sweetheart may give you a hard time, keeping you guessing and making you wonder what your future may be. This is most likely to be a boy-friend or girl-friend you have been going with for quite a while, and who may now feel that the relationship is getting stale.

Even within a stable relationship there could be some aggro and irritation. You may tease each other, and Cancer men in particular may feel that their women folk are asserting themselves too much!

August
Key Dates

Text in *italics* applies to everyone in the world.
Predictions in roman type apply to you alone.

Wednesday 1st: *Excellent day for resolving problems in love. Money matters can also be sorted out.* The day brings luck. Whatever cash you have goes quickly.

Thursday 2nd: *Still a calm, subtle time, with a big emphasis on art, culture and beauty.* Someone may suggest that you go into business together, if only in a part-time way.

Friday 3rd: *A clever day when unexpected answers are found. Not a time to hang back – better to press forward.* There could be a small breakage at home.

Saturday 4th: *A bloody-minded weekend for some, with frustration and tempers flying.* You will feel neglected, especially by a partner who spends evenings in the same way.

Sunday 5th: *A muddled weekend, with imagination running high, and people getting things out of proportion.* A friend may soon be on the move. Be wary of exotic dishes.

Monday 6th: *Still an obstinate time when there could be an explosion of rage. Definitely a down day for many.* It looks like a long day at work. You must do something for nothing.

Tuesday 7th: *People are still at odds with each other, and plans may backfire or be cancelled.* A domestic gadget could go haywire. You will have to rearrange your plans.

Wednesday 8th: *A happier time for many people, with a touch of romance in the air. Harsh words will soon be forgotten.* An official decision will go in your favour. An older person may give you a present, or promise you a treat.

Thursday 9th: *Fairly pleasant, but some people may be depressed and others feel they are getting a raw deal.* Work now, play later. Get your head down and no day-dreaming.

Friday 10th: *People are coming to terms with their situation. Not a wildly happy time.* Plan this weekend as a special time for the family. You feel prosperous, even if you haven't any money.

Saturday 11th: *An active weekend when plenty gets done. People feel dynamic and competitive.* You must be thrifty in one way, but can splurge out somewhere else.

Sunday 12th: *A great time for starting something new, but there is a danger of blowing a fuse.* A little ill-health could put you off some amorous bedtime loving.

Monday 13th: *A blissfully lucky time for some, with a chance of a real surprise out of the blue.* You need some time away from others, so don't plan too busy a social schedule. One friendship will prosper, though.

Tuesday 14th: *Quite a hard-working time and plenty can be achieved. People feel lucky and confident.* You could get into a muddle over romance, especially if you have two sweethearts.

Wednesday 15th: *A slightly edgy day when everything goes fine until...* You will benefit with someone else's tips. Your own intuition isn't too good.

Thursday 16th: *An enjoyable time when work goes well and people feel like taking a small risk.* You notice a mistake – but are you brave enough to point it out?

Friday 17th: *A wise day when sensible decisions are reached and people exercise good judgment.* Travel plans may get complicated. Anger with a child gets you nowhere.

Saturday 18th: *Basically a happy weekend, though people's affections are changing.* A golden opportunity could be around.

Sunday 19th: *An excellent time to achieve plenty, perhaps on the spur of the moment.* A good friend will say goodbye, but you'll meet again. There could be someone new in your neighbourhood who awakens memories from the past.

Monday 20th: *Some people are caught napping by a sudden turn of events. Others are slow on the uptake.* You're in the mood for fun, but for your partner it's all slap and no tickle!

Tuesday 21st: *Still a deceiving time when things are not quite what they seem. People talk their way out of difficulties.* Actually, you're at other people's beck and call all day.

Wednesday 22nd: *A day when effort will pay off. There could be commercial complications, though.* A business venture may run into troubles, and someone could be planning to interfere.

Thursday 23rd: *Not a bright day. People want to take time off* *and enjoy themselves.* Look through clothes to see how they can be improved – or thrown away.

Friday 24th: *Quite an air of luck, though it may all come to nothing. People may be at cross-purposes.* There could be depressing news affecting a friend. Lucky colour: red.

Saturday 25th: *Much the same – lovely for lazing around doing nothing, awkward if you have to work hard.* There will be cross words, which can be laughed off.

Sunday 26th: *A blissful time for many people when feelings become strong and passionate.* Any bright weather should be making you happy. There's less time than you think to get things done.

Monday 27th: *Slightly more awkward day, but still pleasant enough. Someone may say no to a treasured plan.* Your delay will keep others waiting. Be careful of tools in kitchen, workshop or garden, as you don't want an accident.

Tuesday 28th: *Quite pleasant without being special. It's the start of a lucky period lasting until the weekend.* You'll actually feel better after a good row!

Wednesday 29th: *Very lucky day when you use intuition rather than logic. A group of people may prove obstinate.* At work you enjoy a mild bonus, but at home there's an added expense.

Thursday 30th: *An inventive day when you can find a surprise solution to an awkward problem.* One member of the family won't pull his weight. You may see the power of a lucky number, a charm, or an old proverb.

Friday 31st: *Still lucky, still fortunate – and a chance encounter may lead to plenty of pleasure.* Someone is urging you to act out of character – if this means being more flexible, take heed!

Wise Words for August

The business of being a child interests a child
not at all. Children very rarely play
at being other children.

David Holloway

September
Guide

The first half of September is going to be slightly downbeat, as though you feel autumn is in the air already. There may also be a whiff of jealousy, or is it envy? Either way you feel that someone close to you is getting more than you are.

Later in the month things relax more, but there can be problems in a new area – work, for instance. There could be a question mark over a treasured project, and for some Cancer people you doubt whether your job will survive.

Throughout the month you have a strong sense of perfection. You want things just so, and will worry unduly if they are otherwise. This makes you seem pernickety and irritable at times, and you feel that people may misunderstand you.

WORK. A boss may have some disappointing news. Perhaps a hoped-for order will not materialise, or a re-organisation of the department means less opportunity in the future.

For some Cancer people there could be the fear of redundancy, or at least a blocked path to promotion. Even if you have only recently taken up a new job, there could be doubts about its future existence.

There could also be some unpleasant working conditions this month, caused by dust, noise or other pollution. If you work among heavy machinery, there could be a serious fault that means delays, and temporary arrangements.

HOME. There's something threatening in your neighbourhood, too – perhaps a series of burglaries or vandal attacks, or perhaps a feeling that part of the area is going to the dogs. This needn't be anywhere as melodramatic as it sounds, but it still raises a fear in your mind.

There could be further worry at home, perhaps with a child who won't behave. But if you have given him or her a good upbringing, you must hope that good sense will prevail.

There could also be a bit of aggro between different branches of the family. An uncle or aunt, or grown-up brother or sister, could be creating a bit of trouble.

HEALTH. There could be an early autumn cold, sore throat or aching limbs, especially if you are a bit arthritic. It's nothing serious, but if it continues you will feel like seeing a doctor.

It's just possible that there could be some side-effects to any drug you are taking, which may only materialise now after quite a course of treatment. If you have been pursuing a diet or training programme too vigorously, you may now see that you have got things out of proportion.

MONEY. This is a good month to discuss financial matters. There may not be a large outlay of funds, but you are getting more cautious about future prospects.

With a recent purchase there could be a query leading to a long-drawn-out dispute, especially with a department store that has not given you good service.

LEISURE. Not such a good month for holidays, as you have other things on your mind. If you are going away, you may have to phone home often or keep in touch with your place of work.

It could be a month of friendly arguments. You could join a debating society, or enjoy some public speaking, or take part in amateur dramatics. You could be on a committee deciding what to do, or part of a campaign.

Watch out for: poison around home or garden that gets in the wrong place; a determination to rearrange your sporting habits, having had too much or too little in the recent past; several nice evenings out, perhaps with new neighbours; and a letter from abroad which gets you puzzled.

LOVE. This is a better month in romance. Either an existing relationship has pulled back from the brink, or for some Cancerians, there will be a brand-new friendship to develop.

Anyone new is likely to be quite different from previous sweethearts. He or she could be a real card, a bit of a comic, very lively and unorthodox.

An existing love affair or marriage is calmer now, perhaps as a result of a burst of jealousy. If you make your feelings plain, you can put a stop to any incipient fooling around!

77

September
Key Dates

Text in *italics* applies to everyone in the world.
Predictions in roman type apply to you alone.

Saturday 1st: *Quite an amiable day with good feelings being reinforced by love and affection from others.* TV or radio could play a bigger than usual part in your life. There's luck at the end of the day.

Sunday 2nd: *Quite a sexy time, excellent for existing relationships as well as brand-new ones.* A sweetheart will be loving, not angry, which is a relief.

Monday 3rd: *Something could come out of the closet which had been hidden for a long time.* A day-dream will seem exciting, but won't happen unless you do something about it.

Tuesday 4th: *A splendid day for insight and intuition, artistic creativity and patching up an emotional problem.* You may have to repeat a job that you did earlier.

Wednesday 5th: *A day of quiet, steady progress in commerce, business and practical matters.* A child has a bright idea. If asked for money, make sure you know how it will be spent.

Thursday 6th: *In the midst of practical activity there could be a flash of subtle awareness – almost a spiritual insight.* A vehicle could come to a halt in an awkward spot.

Friday 7th: *The end of a good working week when plenty has been achieved and there is more to look forward to.* Ideally you need some good friends near you. But a muddle over dates could produce a disappointment.

Saturday 8th: *Very creative and lively, with people restless and on the move.* Aim to improve your eating habits, which have been into junk food lately.

Sunday 9th: *Lots of energy around, with people being active in sports, recreation and romance.* Someone goes missing for a while. You can give a lot of joy. Forget your own troubles.

Monday 10th: *One or two financial headaches, but people have the energy to do something about them.* Enjoy yourself today. Even if things are bad, look on the bright side.

Tuesday 11th: *A reassuring time when things settle down and people do the right thing.* Argue with people and you'll get nearer the truth. But don't be surprised if you get hurt.

Wednesday 12th: *Still a sensible, reassuring time. Lots of plans will be made full of hope, idealism and ambition.* Phone friends and make a plan for the weekend.

Thursday 13th: *People should feel pretty good about life. Group activities are favoured.* In your love life you may feel that you are being taken for granted. Well, do something about it!

Friday 14th: *Slightly edgy, manic day when people behave rashly, not always with the best of motives.* There could be damage to clothes, perhaps by sitting in the wrong place.

Saturday 15th: *Quite an explosive time, but in a harmonious way! Great weekend for a surprise party.* You make a big song and dance over nothing! As usual you're standing on your precious dignity, not worrying how others feel.

Sunday 16th: *An easy-going time when everyone gets on well with neighbours, friends and family.* Use your Cancer charm to make friends – and flirt a little.

Monday 17th: *A sweet-natured day when romance is strongly favoured. There's a great air of sympathy.* Events turn in your favour. You may be given a responsibility.

Tuesday 18th: *Plenty of energy, but it may come out in a skew-whiff way. Something comes to an end.* Too much hustle and bustle will wear you out. Aim to have a quiet, relaxing day.

Wednesday 19th: *Broadly a good-humoured time, and very lucky for some people.* There could be some lively gossip to hear. Watch your fingers when chopping or cutting.

Thursday 20th: *The strong possibility of victory continues. There's a successful conclusion.* You need a touch of class today, which needn't cost a lot.

Friday 21st: *There's charm to ease away romantic problems, but not in practical affairs.* The evening can still include a celebration. Lucky colour: red.

Saturday 22nd: *Another happy day where people feel comfortable in the bosom of the family.* A mate at work will be in a stubborn mood. Be neighbourly, and invite someone old or helpless out for a treat.

Sunday 23rd: *Another comfortable, relaxed day when older people get the benefit of the doubt.* An event may occur that will make you feel your age.

Monday 24th: *Not a troubling time, though a deep-seated problem could explode into action.* You could do with a holiday! A lucky evening in store.

Tuesday 25th: *Friendly and merry-making day when people want to let off steam after a period of worry.* One of those crazy mixed-up days when nothing is quite normal.

Wednesday 26th: *Things go well. Easy to get on with new colleagues or acquaintances.* There could be some hard physical work which tires you out.

Thursday 27th: *Excellent time for co-operation and teamwork of all kinds. This should be a sweet, loving day.* A modern marvel isn't so marvellous after all.

Friday 28th: *Excellent day for partnerships and business links, with agreement likely and affection all round.* Make a fuss of your face – trim those eyebrows, soothe your eyes, moisturize your skin.

Saturday 29th: *A more disruptive weekend, though responsibility will get the better of rebelliousness.* You must react quickly to a series of events. If involved in a dangerous sport, make sure you take sensible precautions.

Sunday 30th: *Plans could be disrupted. People feel that they must do something different.* A super loving day. Use your brains this weekend.

Wise Words for September

A committee is an animal with four back legs.
John Le Carré

October
Guide

At some stage this October – perhaps around the second week – you become anxious and fretful again. Exactly how strongly it affects you will remain to be seen; it could be only a vague background worry. At worst, however, you could feel insecure and fearful, perhaps about very little.

In particular you worry that some person or organisation may be gaining too much control over you. This could be a strong-minded partner, a bully of a boss or, I suppose, the law, the government or Fate itself!

But do remember that, under this particular influence, you are inclined to work yourself up into a tizzy, all about little or nothing. The important thing is not to keep these fears to yourself. It will be much better to have a good friend with whom you can talk things over, and best of all you should discount fears, rumours and inner worries.

WORK. The greatest area of worry could be to do with your career. You may find yourself in a situation you don't like, where you seem to be in the power of others. But instead of panic you should be calm and patient and simply wait for circumstances to work themselves out.

It may be not your own job which is on the line, but a dispute at work where you can act as peacemaker in some way.

Two other things to watch for: there could be some petty thievery at work, and you could find that worry affects your overall efficiency.

HOME. There's much better togetherness within the family now. You all seem to be pulling together and if one relative has been a problem in the past he or she will now be quieter and more sensible.

You won't be looking for a lot of bustle around the place. You will welcome peace and privacy, and if you share a flat with friends you may wish you had greater quiet around you.

But this could happen quicker than you think; one flatmate could soon be moving away.

HEALTH. You feel fairly fit and well, though there could be the odd queasy stomach and even palpitating heart. But someone close to you could be more ill, and this could add to your air of anxiety.

There could be some temporary damage to an ear due to a blow or unaccustomed air travel. For some Cancerians there could be kidney trouble, and gout is another possibility.

MONEY. People could keep you waiting, particularly if you are owed money or are claiming compensation for loss or damage. Something you thought would go through without a hitch may have to join a queue.

The worst problem will be if you depend on someone else for your weekly allowance. Cancer housewives may find they cannot get hold of enough money, but won't ask for more.

LEISURE. You aren't in a wildly sociable mood this October, and will enjoy quiet, private pleasures at home or amongst one or two friends.

This means you may back out of one or two invitations, including the chance to join in some charity work. You'll feel that charity begins at home.

Watch out for: a man with a plausible line in chat who won't be good for you in the long run; news from old friends, plus the offer to visit them next year; trouble with a car, and the determination to buy anew – eventually!

LOVE. Things seems quite peaceable. A romance begun a month or two ago will be developing nicely, now that you are seeing more of each other. Someone who seemed a good laugh will actually become more serious, and you will take a greater liking to each other.

Marriage hums along nicely, unless you are in the hands of a rotter who takes but rarely gives.

Even if you feel unhappy with a relationship, you can still have some good times together. During this October there will be several times when you are riding a sexual high, enjoying the passion even if there's not much love there.

82

October
Key Dates

Text in *italics* applies to everyone in the world.
Predictions in roman type apply to you alone.

Monday 1st: *A lucky start to the month, with the tide flowing in the right direction.* A parent will be too nosey for your liking. A spot of luck among the gloom.

Tuesday 2nd: *Still a fortunate time, great for starting new projects, travelling and getting in touch.* There will be a slightly downbeat mood to the day.

Wednesday 3rd: *Good fortune smiles on money, or there's the feeling that luck is just round the corner.* You can team up with another person. Together you can achieve a lot.

Thursday 4th: *A wonderful day for romantic love, family affection and feeling a happy part of a larger group.* Happy day, good for a special event. Be lucky with a horse linked with religion.

Friday 5th: *People are living in fantasy land – but it's quite pleasant! Still a favourable time for partnerships.* A fun day, but someone interferes. Fair day for gambling. You could be lucky with a raffle ticket.

Saturday 6th: *An energetic, lively weekend with the accent on surprise, happiness and a successful outcome.* Be wary of buying expensive goods on impulse.

Sunday 7th: *It's great to be getting on with life, rather than sitting back waiting for life to come your way.* Personal relationships are a bit touchy.

Monday 8th: *A terrific start to the working week, especially if you are in commerce, sales, education or the law.* Day of arguments. Try to stop snapping at people who mean you no harm.

Tuesday 9th: *This should be a pleasant, happy occasion, ideal for partying, having luck and generally feeling pleased with life.* At work you may overhear gossip that could have an effect on your job prospects.

Wednesday 10th: *Still a happy-go-lucky mood, with the belief* *that all is for the best.* A day when you want to stretch your horizons. Make a move to improve a friendship.

Thursday 11th: *Very romantic and dreamy, but people are foolish over money and may want things they can't have.* You're living in a slight world of fantasy.

Friday 12th: *A more realistic time, and people are brought down to earth with a bump.* You worry about earnings. Don't rely on intuition and hunch.

Saturday 13th: *Still a resolute time, but lies are being told and nothing is quite what it seems.* Don't ignore warning signs, especially to do with mechanical equipment.

Sunday 14th: *Quite a pleasant day, though voices are raised in anger at one stage.* You'll be glad to put a decision off for a while. A lazy day, but you aren't up to much.

Monday 15th: *Another lovely few days ahead, with people looking for agreement, love and smiles all round.* There could be a secret to keep. If anything's wrong, pay a visit to the doctor.

Tuesday 16th: *Very warm and good-humoured mood, with people looking for fun and pleasure.* You'll feel pleased. There's happiness at work, with optimism in the air.

Wednesday 17th: *A slightly more serious note is struck, especially if travel plans or business is disrupted.* A specialist hobby goes well. You could soon win a prize.

Thursday 18th: *Still a happy time, though something could happen to disrupt the harmony of a group.* Sex and relationships are bothering you. It's a good time for a heart-to-heart talk with your partner.

Friday 19th: *A day of flair and verve, when luck could come out of nowhere.* Plenty of fun and high spirits. Marvellous family day. Lucky numbers: 3, 8.

Saturday 20th: *This bright, lively mood continues through the weekend. Things are lightweight, amusing.* Keep cool. A temper solves nothing. You feel a bit powerless.

Sunday 21st: *People are on the move. Plans are being made, ideas canvassed – but it may all come to nothing.* You want to go out, but something will hold you up.

Monday 22nd: *Excellent start to the working week, with the emphasis on youth and bright ideas.* Your partner could be in a touchy mood, especially about work.

Tuesday 23rd: *Slightly edgy mood when people want to argue rather than agree. But there's still a positive atmosphere.* You need to get out of a rut – but your partner wants the opposite.

Wednesday 24th: *Very lively and go-ahead, when life seems full of competition. People make the best of a bad job.* Old things will appeal to you. Lots of taste and charm.

Thursday 25th: *A pleasant time, great for seeing friends, writing letters and laying plans for the months ahead.* Children want more than they can have.

Friday 26th: *People feel like taking a financial risk, but will draw back in time. Romance, too, is looking for a bit of a lark.* There's a worry about holidays. Travel is liable to delay.

Saturday 27th: *An interesting day with an unexpected development or two.* There could be a budding romance – also a winner for you in the afternoon's races.

Sunday 28th: *There could be one or two family rows, but it all ends up with titters in the end.* A day of lost tempers, guilty consciences. There are links with your childhood in some way.

Monday 29th: *The start of another lovely week when people should feel very comfortable in each other's company.* A car may still be off the road. You may have to cancel a trip.

Tuesday 30th: *A light, bright, easy and breezy day when people feel that spring is in the air.* Expenses pile up. Could be a stomach upset. Otherwise you'll enjoy being in company.

Wednesday 31st: *Very much the same, with little holding people back from having a good time.* A day of emotional obsession, when your own mood, for better or worse, grips you hard.

Wise Words for October

One should never let one's happiness
depends on other people.
H. Granville Barker

November
Guide

This seems a much better month, as though the tide has turned. You will delight in the good things of life, and feel much more confident about the future.

If anyone issues you with a dare – silly or otherwise – you will respond to it. Altogether you seem much more courageous and positive, so there is likely to have been good news recently.

As a result you seem bonny and bright, and not nearly as depressed as you may have been last month.

Two things to watch for: there could be some exciting family news now or in the near future, and if you are the creative type, you could develop a new enthusiasm that could see you through the next few months.

WORK. Although there may be a setback, it won't affect you personally. If you have been worried about job prospects, they're much brighter now. This is a much better time to be looking for another job, or feeling that your present one is safe.

One reason may be that someone who was giving you trouble has now quietened down or moved away altogether. There is a strong emphasis on teamwork, so you may be working with a new group or joining up with people from another firm or department. Together you could achieve a lot.

HOME. Babies could be much on your mind. If you are a woman you could be pining for a child, or having one, or enjoying the presence of someone else's in the house. So you could become a grandparent, or a toddler from next door will keep toddling in!

The fabric of your home may need some attention. If you only rent, you could have difficulty in getting a landlord to put things right. If you own outright, you will be given several quotes, and you shouldn't necessarily pick the cheapest. Go for the most thorough workmanship.

HEALTH. It wouldn't be surprising if toxins that have built up

86

in your body need to get out this month – either through a boil, a fever or inflammation of some kind. You could feel quite wretched for a few days, but it won't last long.

Some Cancer people may have got so depressed in October that you can't lift yourself from it now. It could have been the last straw, so to speak. But there really is no need, so you really must hitch your waggon to a star, so to speak, and lift yourself from any gloom that was around.

MONEY. You must re-jig your budget to take account of a big new expense looming. This could be to do with house repairs, an extension, perhaps a new house altogether – or maybe a car.

The trouble is that you may spend time with someone with more cash than sense, and you may get into the habit of watching extravagance at work!

LEISURE. You do become more sociable this month – and some people may have thought that you were out of circulation altogether. Now's your chance to give a party of your own, go to one or two other functions, enjoy a meal out and generally get back into the social swim.

People may be urging you to join a club, which is quite a good idea provided it is a genuinely recreational organisation and won't involve you in a lot of hard work.

Watch out for: lots of laughter amongst people of your own sex; a sports event that wouldn't normally appeal, but does now; and a chance to press ahead with some artistic activity – either something entirely new or a craft or skill you have been practising for years.

LOVE. You feel much more bouncy now, in yourself, but your love life itself may not greatly improve. Within an existing courtship that seemed to be going well there could now be one or two doubts – perhaps on both sides. This doesn't mean the end of the relationship, but you are both pausing and thinking.

A long-term relationship will be jogging along nicely, without any big problems. There could be one tiny moment of jealousy again, but it isn't crucial and you will soon forget it.

There are good links with Gemini and Sagittarius people, but not so good with Aquarius or Aries.

November
Key Dates

Text in *italics* applies to everyone in the world.
Predictions in roman type apply to you alone.

Thursday 1st: *Another interesting, lively day with a strong accent on love and social life.* You have strong feelings, but keep them to yourself.

Friday 2nd: *Even better – a great evening for a party or a special romantic date.* There could be a clever move you can make. Good for finance. If you look at a money problem carefully, you'll see what must be done.

Saturday 3rd: *A terrific weekend, though some people may have to think long and hard before making up their minds.* A youngster pleases you, and seems to be growing up nicely.

Sunday 4th: *Another swooning day when romance is all you could wish for.* There could be a budding romance. Health should be blooming.

Monday 5th: *Plenty of fun and good fortune in the air, with people eager to have a good time.* Happy working day, with no real problems. Lucky numbers: 5, 9.

Tuesday 6th: *A strong air of good fortune, whether in sport or business. Things just seem to fall into place.* Another cold could catch you unawares. Your partner is grumpy. You may go off a lover who has behaved badly.

Wednesday 7th: *If things have been undecided up till now, there could be a happy conclusion to everything.* A clear-headed day. You'll be annoyed with people who are vague.

Thursday 8th: *A key date for some relationships, with things at a make-or-break level.* You want to take life easy, but there's a special job you must tackle.

Friday 9th: *Still a crucial time in relationships, with the emphasis broadly happy and long-lasting.* Not an easy day as far as children are concerned. One may be ill, another fractious.

Saturday 10th: *Things that have been repressed may come out* *into the open. A testing time.* Excellent time to learn something new – about health in particular.

Sunday 11th: *Quite a crucial weekend, with some people feeling under pressure and others exerting the pressure!* A day of friendly arguments. Look for a new way of doing something familiar.

Monday 12th: *Excellent time for meetings, discussions and agreements. People need a break in the evening.* Get your head down to neglected paperwork. If there has been ill-will, this will now disappear.

Tuesday 13th: *A hard-working but successful time when detailed knowledge and hard work pays good dividends.* You could suddenly start a new romance. You'll be lucky with a bet. Watch for a jockey or horse beginning with S.

Wednesday 14th: *Much the same, with plenty being achieved. It's worth making a big effort.* A day when you're slightly at odds with the people around you.

Thursday 15th: *A slightly more surprising time, when things that haven't been thought of start to develop.* You are busy making plans for the future. Lucky time in the post?

Friday 16th: *No big problems, people want to forget their worries and have a good time.* You could get slightly ill through over- exertion. Be careful if playing sport.

Saturday 17th: *A more explosive mixture, with people quarrelling on the spur of the moment.* Ideal day for mixing with a close friend who can put you straight on a few things.

Sunday 18th: *Still a quarrelsome mood in the air, but it's easier to pour oil on troubled waters.* There could be a budding romance. You feel emotionally insecure for a while. You may be anxious on someone else's behalf.

Monday 19th: *A more loving mood again, especially within the family circle. There could be financial surprises.* You will get things out of proportion. Beware of allowing the past to influence your future plans.

Tuesday 20th: *Money ups and downs continue, and people should be feeling positive and warm-hearted.* You stay distant, while someone wants you to become more involved.

Wednesday 21st: *A mild day with nobody pushed too much in one direction or another. There's a pleasant mood of*

89

co-operation. Nice romantic date, especially if you haven't seen each other for a while.

Thursday 22nd: *Things become more lively and uncertain. There is a risk of taking things too hurriedly.* A sociable day. A trip with friends will be fine.

Friday 23rd: *Some depression and worry, but people gain from the activities of a group helping them.* There could be some cheating you do not approve of.

Saturday 24th: *A surprisingly sexy day when people want to indulge themselves. Not a puritanical time!* You take great pride in your home. You feel slightly nervous in strange company. But you should be surrounded by warmth and friendliness.

Sunday 25th: *Quite lively and interesting, but there may be a few black moods around.* You may be kept waiting. An argument with an older relative.

Monday 26th: *People can't leave well alone. All sorts of little problems could be coming to the surface.* If you're taking a winter break, this could be an exciting moment in your holiday.

Tuesday 27th: *The aggressive mood continues. Some people are pushing too hard, causing pain to others.* Your partner is in a weird mood. You may get snappish and surly.

Wednesday 28th: *Things come to a head, with heads being knocked together. Stay out of the kitchen if you can't stand the heat!* Excellent day for reaching business decisions.

Thursday 29th: *A much happier time, with luck, happiness and good fortune breaking out of nowhere.* If you give children too much love, they will shy away.

Friday 30th: *The good mood continues, with Venus and Jupiter bringing happiness to many.* Steady day at work, but mayhem at home! It's swings and roundabouts – you gain in one direction only to lose in another!

Wise Words for November

Inexperience is what makes a young man do
what an older man says is impossible.

Herbert V. Prochow

December
Guide

You end the year in high spirits – hard-working but good-humoured and really starting to look forward to the New Year.

You go through a great chatterbox phase, wanting to stay in touch, spread ideas, rumours and gossip, and perhaps, more seriously, putting things down on paper.

There will certainly be a sigh of relief if a problem is solved or a danger passed. In some way you may be going back to an original plan, after working out lots of other possibilities.

WORK. Your standing may go up several notches, and there could be the promise of extra pay or promotion soon. If you are having trouble with an immediate boss, people higher up are going to be more pleased with you.

For some Cancer people it will be a day-dreamy time, planning out the next course of action. This applies particularly if you run your own business or are thinking of starting up a new business in the New Year.

There could be a last-minute emergency just before the Christmas break, but working a few unsocial hours will be worthwhile.

HOME. There's good news to do with some belongings that have been lost or mislaid. If you have been waiting for an insurance payout, it will arrive, and you may get the thumbs up from a spouse for some new furniture.

You may not like the friends that a child is making, but will realise that you can't control their lives for ever. Otherwise Christmas preparations go well, and you may be more extravagant than usual with presents, decorations, food and drink. You also have a better relationship with friends and neighbours living nearby, and altogether you have a happier Christmas than in recent years.

HEALTH. Broadly speaking you are strong and vigorous at the turn of the year, and have nothing much to worry about, except in the third week when you could be poorly. But it

91

won't last long, and you should be fit and fine for the party season.

But your digestion is not as good as it can be, and I should be careful of rich and spicy foods which might give you a little trouble over the holiday.

MONEY. There could be a rebate coming your way, and also the chance to earn a little extra. This may not happen until the New Year, but you can plan for it now.

Shopping goes well, unless you are relying on mail order goods arriving in time for Christmas. Deliveries are likely to be slow, and something could get lost in the post altogether.

I think you are in an extravagant mood and cash will slip through your fingers like brandy butter! In the Christmas or New Year sales take care where you put a purse or wallet.

LEISURE. Once you get your bounce back there'll be no stopping you. You are determined to enjoy yourself in the party season, and all low spirits will be forgotten.

But one set of friends may be fun one moment and a nuisance the next. You may have to keep them – or gate-crashers – away from a particular party of your own, and you may not want friends and family to mix all that much.

Team spirit is quite important, and if you are taking part in any kind of performance or sports event this month your group will do well.

Watch out for: a child's entertainment that will be great fun; a new music stand that really grabs you; a lovely offer that you are going to have to turn down; and lots of resolutions to enjoy yourself more in 1991.

LOVE. Your good-humoured mood means that you can swing a bad-tempered partner out of irritability and moodiness. If there is always a power struggle in your marriage, this time you will come out on top.

You are so busy with work, society and entertaining that you may not have too much time for a love life as such. But your sexy moments will be quite pleasant, and a slightly dodgy love affair will come back on course during December.

December
Key Dates

Text in *italics* applies to everyone in the world.
Predictions in roman type apply to you alone.

Saturday 1st: *An amusing, cheap and cheerful day when people want to enjoy themselves.* An ultra-cautious day. You are worried about getting things wrong, or having a small accident.

Sunday 2nd: *Still pleasant and enterprising, with lots of warmth in marriage or love affair.* Co-operation is the keyword of the day. There could be a touch of ill-health. Friends will help.

Monday 3rd: *Still a warm-hearted time with people sociable, sensual and self-indulgent. Not a fussy time.* There will be a friendly argument with a lover. You want fun, but your sweetheart wants privacy.

Tuesday 4th: *A comfortable day when people are out for what they can get. One or two people get hurt.* A lie may be told. You won't want to reveal your true heartfelt emotions.

Wednesday 5th: *A super time when good fortune shines on many people. A great time for travel.* A memory from the past gives you an idea for the future.

Thursday 6th: *Still lucky, with no real hold-ups on the road to pleasure.* Children will be inquisitive. A bitter-sweet time. There could be a loss, but there's a consolation in your emotional life.

Friday 7th: *An itsy-bitsy sort of day with nothing much happening. People worry about money.* Plans go through without a murmur. You handle a complicated situation with grace and tact.

Saturday 8th: *An amusing day when people want to try something out of the ordinary.* You may be tempted to stray. What starts as an innocent flirtation becomes a matter of strong feelings.

Sunday 9th: *Another lively day when no one is particularly tactful, wise or cautious.* You still feel sensitive, and are scared of taking any kind of risk.

Monday 10th: *People can find their way round difficulties, which is nice for them but a bit disruptive for others.* You must work when you don't want to. Another indication that you'll do well by taking care, using common sense, etc.

Tuesday 11th: *An upbeat day when people are looking to the future, not the past. Old sores will be forgotten.* A nice family day, with fresh air and perhaps a special treat.

Wednesday 12th: *People are bubbling with enthusiasm, which will upset anyone who is depressed.* You have to pick the lesser of two evils. A drink at a pub is great fun.

Thursday 13th: *No big worries, but it's still an indiscreet, sensual and slightly greedy time.* A sense of discipline comes to the fore. You may have to make a sacrifice – in love?

Friday 14th: *An extravagant day, excellent for showing hospitality to others.* More friendly. Good for business. If you're worrying about the family budget, one of you will want to spend, and the other will want to save.

Saturday 15th: *Still a warm-hearted time – great for family affairs, romantic meetings.* If you're seriously ill yourself, this could be a day of decision – but a favourable one.

Sunday 16th: *Slightly more depressing time, when people may fall ill just before Christmas.* You are intensely independent at the moment. You will want to go your own way.

Monday 17th: *Another harum-scarum day when people do not want to conform – they're all for a bit of diversity.* Good time to be on holiday. A bet to do with home, family or yourself will probably win. Worth trying, anyway.

Tuesday 18th: *Nice and lively, when nobody wants to be too serious or down in the mouth.* Excellent day, though you may be happier on your own than always in company.

Wednesday 19th: *Terrific fun provided you're prepared to let your hair down.* Excellent day for family business. You achieve a lot, and everyone will eventually be pleased.

Thursday 20th: *Another marvellous day if you're unconventional, looking for madcap fun.* Links with an older person are strong and loyal. Friends are planning a scheme you don't like.

Friday 21st: *Still a strong party mood, excellent for get-*

togethers and social functions. In a romance there's peace, after a period of doubt. A moody day, which is unusual for you.

Saturday 22nd: *A lucky day for some, and an extravagant one for others.* Beware of seeming too vain. Happy hours between the generations. Good for a celebration.

Sunday 23rd: *Some more splendid influences, especially if you're the spiritual type.* It's tempting to escape responsibilities. Leave your troubles behind and go somewhere different.

Monday 24th: *Another helter-skelter day when people are restless, on the move and searching.* Your partner is in a weird mood. You may get snappish and surly.

Tuesday 25th: *Not a quiet, passive day. Excellent for parties, and everyone seems on the move.* You'll want to steer a child in one direction, but I doubt whether you'll be successful.

Wednesday 26th: *Still an enjoyable day, but the merry-making may catch up with people!* Someone is short of cash.

Thursday 27th: *Excellent time for putting differences behind you. There's lots of friendship.* Changeable moods. Bad news in the afternoon. Children are an extra burden.

Friday 28th: *Good for travel, having fun – but not so good if you're handling money.* You are suspicious about someone else's motives. Perhaps you aren't being told the whole truth.

Saturday 29th: *Still good for travel, and the romantic are living in cloud-cuckoo land!* You supply a lot of energy to your friendships. They look to you for amusement and driving-force.

Sunday 30th: *There could be a little mental depression for some, but most people feel it's a time for letting rip!* There could be an argument with neighbours, but is it worth all the bother?

Monday 31st: *A stunning end to the year, with a Sun-Uranus conjunction making it a day of fireworks.* Plenty of charm and intelligence today, so you'll be a success with others.

Wise Words for December

Honest criticism is hard to take,
particularly from a relative,
a friend, an acquaintance or a stranger.
Franklin P.Jones

All Futura Books are available at your bookshop or
newsagent, or can be ordered from the following address:
Futura Books, Cash Sales Department,
P.O. Box 11, Falmouth, Cornwall TR10 9EN.

Please send cheque or postal order (no currency), and
allow 60p for postage and packing for the first book
plus 25p for the second book and 15p for each additional
book ordered up to a maximum charge of £1.90 in U.K.

B.F.P.O. customers please allow 60p for
the first book, 25p for the second book plus 15p per
copy for the next 7 books, thereafter 9p per book

Overseas customers, including Eire, please allow £1.25
for postage and packing for the first book, 75p for the
second book and 28p for each subsequent title ordered.